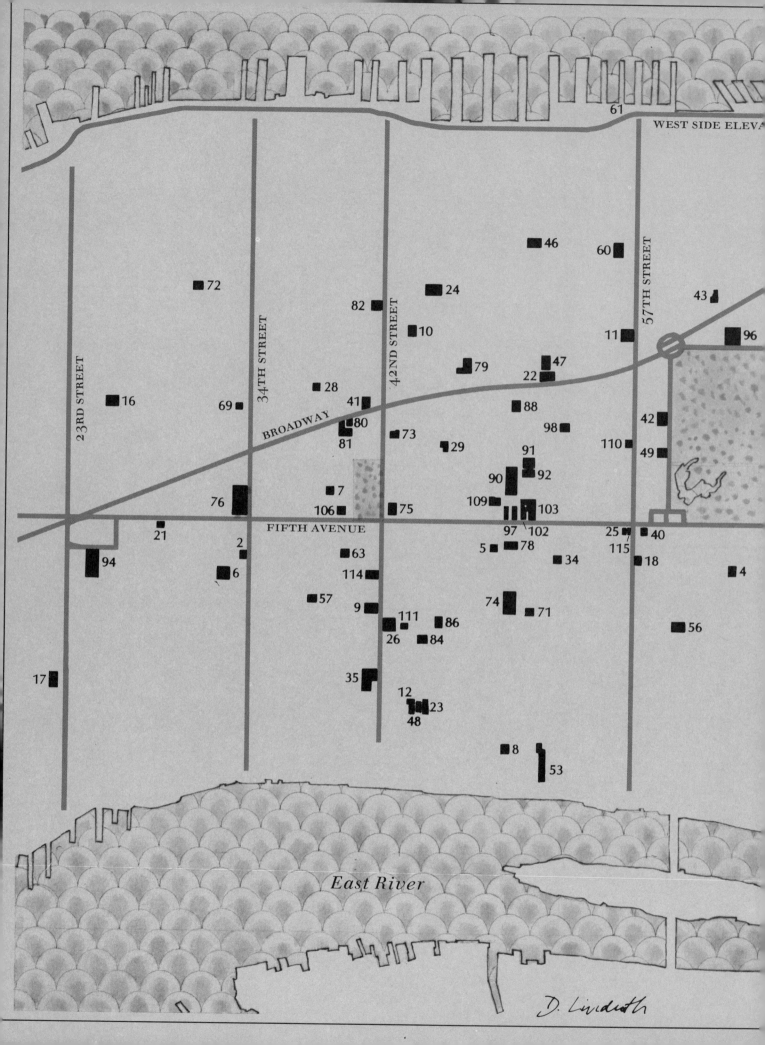

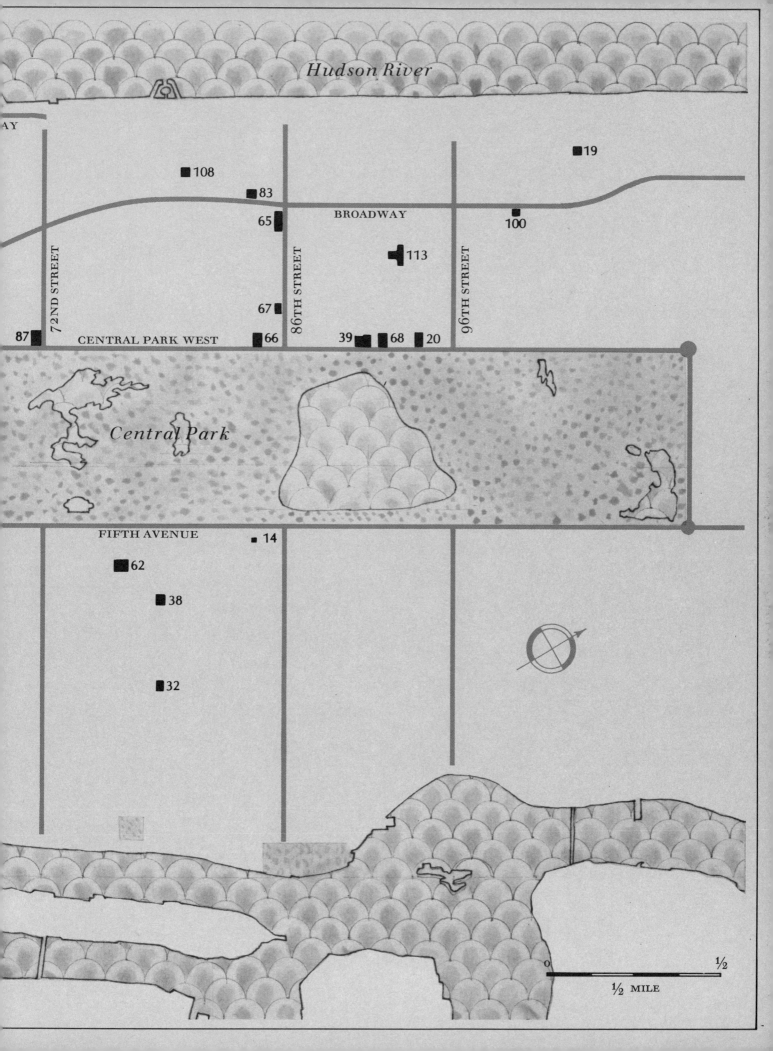

Hudson River

108

19

83

BROADWAY

65

100

72ND STREET

86TH STREET

113

96TH STREET

67

87   CENTRAL PARK WEST   66   39   68   20

Central Park

FIFTH AVENUE   14

62

38

32

0   ½
              ½ MILE

SKYSCRAPER STYLE

26. CHRYSLER BUILDING (overleaf)

A. The stainless steel on the cresting of this skyscraper of 1928-30 designed by William Van Alen is actually mounted on wooden forms (not visible) which were prepared in a shipyard.

SKYSCRAPER STYLE

Art Deco New York

CERVIN ROBINSON
ROSEMARIE HAAG BLETTER

 New York   OXFORD UNIVERSITY PRESS   1975

Copyright © 1975 by Oxford University Press
Library of Congress Catalogue Card Number: 74-22885
Printed in the United States of America

PREFACE

In the last quarter century architectural historians have turned their attention to a number of past periods ranging from Italian Renaissance to High Victorian, from Shingle Style to Art Nouveau. Subsequently Modern architects who read them have commendably aimed to adopt into their own discipline what seemed the strengths of some of these styles of the past, whether these were Renaissance modular principles or Victorian naturalism. At the same time there has always been some suspicion that architects, instead of adopting the principles, were still merely copying the surface appearances of styles. We might say therefore that this book is not intended as a pattern-book.

Its subject is precisely what, in the thirties, the proponents of the International Style were revolting against in America. It was this Beaux-Arts architecture of the skyscraper which then seemed, of all architectures, the one which least understood the direction in which the twentieth century should go. Ultimately the International Style did in some ways succeed in being the antithesis it meant to be; in others it now looks surprisingly to have been the same job done to a different and more successful sales pitch.

The authors might have chosen to show what seemed the best of Art Deco architecture throughout the U.S. If they had, the book would have been little more than an amused once-over-lightly. It aims instead to point to the intentions of the architects who practiced Art Deco as well as to the sources of the style and to illustrate the wealth of buildings that New York City, the epitome of the Art Deco metropolis, its Gotham, still possesses. The book does not say everything about architecture in New York between the wars; it will not have the last word on the style. It aims instead to be an introduction to the study of Art Deco architecture.

The authors' interest in the subject was first aroused in the sixties: one of us took a photograph in 1966 of three of the buildings this book deals with, a view from the roof of the Seagram Building which has long since been closed off by new construction. This picture appeared in *Architectural Forum* at the end of that year and appears here as the frontispiece to the first essay. The other author turned her attention to these New York buildings in 1968 while in the process of doing a research paper on Expressionism in American architecture as part of a doctoral program in the Columbia Art History Department. Thereafter, because of other commitments, we did not immediately pursue the subject. In the years that followed, some books and articles on Art Deco appeared. Most treated architecture tangentially—the exception being David Gebhard's work on the West Coast Moderne. We resumed our work on Art Deco architecture in 1971 when the John Simon Guggenheim Memorial Foundation gave a grant under which the pictures for the book could be taken.

The authors are indebted to others besides the Foundation for help of many kinds in the preparation of the book . . . above all to Alfred Frazer for suggesting it to us in the first place and especially to James F. O'Gorman and Edgar Kaufmann, Jr., who were kind enough to read the text at, respectively, an early and a late stage in its writing; also to Reyner Banham, Peter Blake, James Marston Fitch, Adolf K. Placzek, and G. E. Kidder Smith; to William H. Jordy, E. J. Kahn, Jr., Henry-Russell Hitchcock, George R. Collins, Philip C. Johnson, Rockwell K. DuMoulin, Kenneth Frampton, Wallace K. Harrison, Mrs. Liselotte Kahn, Herbert Lippmann, Robert Djerejian, George E. Thomas, and Ludwig Glaeser; to the following institutions and their staffs: first and foremost the Avery Architectural Library at Columbia —especially to Neville Thompson, the New York Public Library, the library of the New York Historical Society, the New York Chapter of the A.I.A., and the National Institute for Architectural Education; and finally to Sebastian Mazzola and his staff at the Plan Desk of the City Department of Buildings, whose records and help are always so valuable to research in Manhattan.

New York   C. R.
October 1974   R. H. B.

CONTENTS

SKYSCRAPER STYLE

BUILDINGS AND ARCHITECTS

Major sections of New York City—the financial district, the midtown area, Central Park West, and Washington Heights, not to speak of Ocean Parkway in Brooklyn and Grand Concourse in the Bronx—are studded with buildings done in a style which few have bothered to notice until recently. With the exception of a few examples like the News and McGraw-Hill buildings, which were considered just short of International Style, the Empire State because it was the world's tallest building, or Rockefeller Center because of its ambitious program, these structures, which had gone up in the late twenties and the thirties, had become pariahs of modern architecture. Seen in the light of the purist ethic of the Modern Movement, their gaudy efflorescence of color and ornament looked gauche. But in America of the late twenties and thirties Art Deco was the overwhelmingly prevailing modernism. The European International Style that had developed by the late thirties was not widely applied in America. Today, when we have had twenty years of the austere architecture ushered in by Skidmore, Owings & Merrill's Lever House, it may be refreshing to re-examine an architecture that aims to be popular, entertaining, and urbane.

The prevalent New York City architecture of the twenties and thirties also, in fact, reflects an international style, one that for a time was much more widely accepted than *the* International

Gotham: the spire of the Chrysler Building (William Van Alen, 1928-30), seen between the RCA Victor tower, left (Cross & Cross, 1930-31) and one of the towers of the Waldorf-Astoria, right (Schultze & Weaver, 1930-31).

Style. Images of some of these buildings, like the Waldorf-Astoria, the Chrysler and the RCA Victor buildings, or the Empire State, helped crystallize our image of Gotham, the city of skyscrapers and urban chic, without which such a film as *King Kong* would be difficult to imagine. The distinctive forms of the Chrysler and Empire State have assumed the familiar characteristics of landmarks, an associational value in which they will not easily be replaced by the twin shafts of the World Trade Center. Many of these buildings are well worth taking a second look at before they disappear from our rapidly changing cityscape. Smaller stores and restaurants have long since gone. But such larger projects too as the Ziegfeld Theater, the House of Detention for Women, and a series of pier buildings have gone in the last few years, and the McGraw-Hill Building awaits a somewhat uncertain future.

Art Deco appeared on the Main Streets of towns large and small in America, but it was first of all a style of the large cities. Used for a wide variety of urban building types, it was primarily a commercial style. It was thought by American architects, and with some justification, to be an international style and one in which, by the second half of the twenties, they had achieved preeminence because of their skyscrapers[1]—a building type much admired in Europe but not much built there until after World War II. In America there was some ambivalence about the skyscraper. If it was America's great achievement, it was also only justifiable in areas with the highest land values,[2] and the prime example of such an area was New York City.

There are several standards by which one can judge the impact of an architecture. One can look at its direct stylistic influence on subsequent architecture, as we have done with the International Style. If that is the standard, Art Deco has had (so far) just about no influence at all. Or one can look at its impact on the cities in which it occurs. Paris, for instance, has scarcely been affected by the buildings Le Corbusier built there in the twenties and thirties. Berlin was decisively affected by its early Modern buildings; Amsterdam more so. And the impact of Art Deco on New York City was greater still.

Architectural criticism can ask what intentions lie behind a building, and then (provided the intentions are not irresponsible) can ask to what extent they have been fulfilled. Stated most briefly, the occasion for Art Deco in New York City was a building boom that started in 1925 and lasted until 1931; and the intention of New York architects was to unite several separate ideas in the design of the skyscrapers called for in the boom years. The buildings they designed were marked by European decorative influences but were also affected by certain ideas from Chicago, by the theater, and by an image of a future New York that had long had popular currency. The career of this architecture was probably also determined by the fact that its journalism was weak. Finally, it was marked, and perhaps most significantly, by the training that New York architects had received.

Education

The Beaux-Arts educational system was criticized in the 1930s and after as an ingrown, Francophile system which put the handling of India ink on stretched paper above training in building and had its students designing the most useless of monumental buildings, and in styles of the past. But, however monumental these student projects were, the buildings involved were meant as public amenities; their grandeur was intended to be both accessible to the general public and comprehensible to it. These were qualities the Art Deco skyscrapers would have. Student projects were supposed to surmount simply utilitarian needs: "It is sometimes necessary," wrote John Harbeson in the twenties, "to add interest to a plan composed almost entirely of useful rooms; at such times one's ingenuity is given a real test."[3] As for style, architects trained under this system can sound downright hapless with regard to that. This is Raymond M. Hood (1881-1934, MIT, Ecole des Beaux-Arts[4]):

My experience, which in reality consists of designing only two skyscrapers [the Tribune tower and the American Radiator Company building], does not justify my expressing an opinion as to whether a building should be treated vertically, horizontally or in cubist fashion. On the contrary, it has convinced me that on these matters I should not have a definite opinion. To use these two buildings as examples, they are both in the "vertical" style or what is called "Gothic," simply because I happened to make them so. If at the time of designing them I had been under the spell of Italian campaniles or Chinese pagodas, I suppose the resulting compositions would have been "horizontal." . . . Nothing but harm could result if at this stage in our development the free exercise of study and imagination should stop, and the standardizing and formulating of our meager knowledge and experience should now take its place.

It might be proper to say something precise about the different styles, but I am as much in the air about style as I am about everything else.[5]

Perhaps the aspect of Beaux-Arts training that was of most significance to design in the late twenties and the thirties was the special order and manner in which student projects were done.

The student started with an *esquisse,* a sketch made at the beginning of a project in which he committed himself to a general form for his solution. "It is done in a short and fixed time, usually nine hours, and is made 'en loge.' This means literally 'in the box' or booth . . . the spirit of this requirement is that the student shall make his sketch without the aid of books or advice."[6] Then, "in the development of a problem, the elements indicated in the esquisse (rooms or open spaces in plan, motives in elevation), may be changed considerably in proportion, but no such elements may be left out, and none may be added."[7] Thus the most important decisions were made at the beginning of design and without any give and take among fellow students. The rest was filling in. The major student projects were organized as competitions at which students were not present to defend their drawings. In the atelier criticisms were eventually given, but were clearly one-sided affairs: "A man who is a good architectural critic is apt to be temperamental—most talented people are. A temperamental man is not always at his best—his moods fluctuate, and so does his efficiency, as his spirit is buoyant or depressed. . . . It is for this reason that it is well at the very beginning to form habits of preparing things for the critic with an eye to his comfort."[8] So the architect was taught to show his cards at the beginning of the game; and his training included neither collaboration nor verbal defense of his designs.

The original esquisse, if properly done, committed the student to a great deal, but the details were left purposely vague. This was not an architecture in which carefully thought out detail could be multiplied to make a whole. The esquisse approach presumably accounts furthermore for a lack of connection between the mass of some Art Deco buildings and their detail. It also explains how, once a French exposition, the 1925 Paris Exposition Internationale des Arts Décoratifs et Industriels Modernes, had signaled to French-trained and Francophile American architects that modernism was now acceptable in France, a variety of modern decorative influences could fall into place like the last piece that would complete the puzzle of the New York skyscraper style, Art Deco.

Design in the Early Twenties

The shape which New York buildings took once the boom started was influenced both by a design which the Finn Eliel Saarinen had submitted to a competition held in 1922 for a new

Eliel Saarinen, Chicago Tribune Building competition entry, 1922.

Chicago Tribune Building[9] and by a New York zoning ordinance passed in 1916 which required building setbacks. Saarinen's highly regarded entry was taken to be style-less and was thought in the twenties finally to have freed architects from what had seemed the inevitable alternatives in skyscraper design, Gothic solutions on the one hand and vertically stretched Classical ones on the other.[10] New York Art Deco skyscraper design started off on the Saarinen model, which was then repeatedly modified in response to the zoning law. This law required setbacks, which were to start at a height dependent on the width of the street, and allowed a tower of unlimited height on part of the building site; it was understood to encourage a certain shape of building: a ziggurat-crowned prism surmounted by a tower or two towers side by side. Architects had high hopes in the early twenties that it would transform their city desirably; but because of the law's complexity and because building activity did not pick up for some years after the war, the precise shape of things to come was uncertain even as late as 1924. As a result of interest in the law's ultimate effect there appeared in the architectural journals of the day a number of articles on the subject; at least seven were printed in the first half of the twenties.[11]

Of these the most interesting to the present-day reader is one published in 1923, which illustrated the results of a study by the firm of Helmle & Corbett of the building shape which the zoning law would encourage on a full New York City block.[12] The results were drawn in perspective by the professional renderer Hugh Ferriss (1889-1962, Washington University). In one rendering the maximum shape allowed by the law was shown, its tower rising into the clouds (Fig. 1). Then a series of modifications of this "envelope" were given, made with the exigencies of daylight (Fig. 2) and the realities of steel-frame construction (Fig. 3) and of rental (Fig. 4) in mind. A further rendering (not illustrated here) showed the final, logically arrived at shape given an "architectural" treatment by the application of columns to its base and crown (a treatment apparently not recommended by the architects but offered out of fair-mindedness). A final drawing showed how the Manhattan of the future would look when such buildings had been widely built.

This high hope of things to come from a zoning law is alien to us. Since World War II we have looked to the architect to be mostly in control of his work, though we know he may have to compromise here and there. In the twenties, however, circumstances seem to have been expected to play a larger role. An ar-

Figure 1

Figure 2

Figure 3

Figure 4

Helmle & Corbett, zoning envelope studies, renderings by Hugh Ferriss.

chitect would apologize for the top of his building because he had rushed in the design of it: "When the 17th story masonry work was being built, we were still studying the top of the building at ½″ scale. I merely insert this to ask for a little indulgence on the part of people who might otherwise be inclined to be very critical of the result."[13] Or a critic would say that the top of a building had been improvised at the last moment when considerable evidence was available that this was simply not so.[14] Design both then and now may well in reality be made up of a similar mixture of intention and compromise; but it was certainly considered to be more at the mercy of circumstance then.[15]

One reason for this feeling that events were out of control was a radical change in architectural practice. Architects trained to build monumental buildings such as theaters, embassies, and city halls, found themselves in the second half of the twenties in the midst of a commercial building boom which required maximum rental space and immediate return on investment. In 1927 Edwin Avery Park wrote:

If the question be asked "What is architecture in this country today?" one can only answer it is not what it once was. It certainly is not what it was, say ten years ago. Times have changed and many architects heave sighs. There is no more fun in the game. . . . The architect might as well never have wasted his time learning to design. His job is now that of financial engineer, his time spent in cutting, scraping and shoe-horning, trying to produce something, without time to worry too much over how the thing will look. . . . Art and architecture no longer function upon a basis of patronage. Architecture is competing in the great modern struggle to survive through fitness.[16]

The steel structure of the buildings put up in the late twenties and early thirties was accepted as something given. But finding the proper form of cladding for a skeleton frame was felt to be a major task. For this architects turned to a source of design outside architecture and to a theory. The first was stage design, which in the twenties had an importance that now, when both television and set-less motion pictures compete with theater, it no longer has. The theory, a German one that the forms for the parts of a building should be derived from the parts of original, that is, primitive buildings (in particular, that the proper form for a wall was that of a woven mat), presumably came to New York architects by way of Chicago, along with the skeleton frame.[17] In New York Art Deco, forms taken directly from the theater appear in lobbies and at building entrances, or the lower floors of high buildings are given forms like painted sets facing onto the street. On other buildings the cladding of steel frames is given a fabric pattern or a woven form, or in some cases looks explicitly like hanging curtains. The designer and writer Paul T. Frankl (1887-1958) referred to such walls as "brick tapestries hung from the sky."[18] In a number of ways the Art Deco had the characteristic of being an architecture of "both-and." Decorative forms, for instance, might be both primitive and modern or both traditional and exotic. The top of a building could be both pagoda-form and a frozen fountain,[19] and the architecture would thereby seem either the richer in meaning, or the more imprecise in intention.

When twenties architects considered dealing with sections of the city larger than single buildings, the ideal of a city with multilevel traffic arteries appealed to them. A multilevel solution to the city's traffic problems was proposed in 1923 to the Regional Plan Association by a committee chaired by Harvey Wiley Corbett (1873-1954, University of California, Ecole des Beaux-Arts). Pedestrians were to pass through shopping arcades at the second-story level of the city's buildings. These arcades were to be connected by bridges crossing the roadways between. Automobile traffic would be at ground level; parking might cover the whole of the area under the city's buildings if that proved necessary. Underpasses were to occur at major intersections, and rail traffic would be underground. Though such visions as this had a popular ancestry in the frontispieces to Moses King's *Views of New York* published before the First World War, the committee's image, it claimed in its report, was that of Venice:

From an architectural viewpoint and regard to form, decoration, and proportion, the idea presents all the loveliness, and more, of Venice. . . . Venice is the adaptation of a city to the necessities of the terrain on which it is built. The New York of the future will be an adaptation of the metropolis to the needs of traffic, freeing the city from the unsightly congestion and turmoil of the present. Pedestrians will move about through the arcaded streets, out of danger from traffic, protected from the snows of winter and the glare of the summer sun. Walking would become a pastime. . . . Shopping would be a joy.[20]

Fragments of this multilevel image appeared in several Art Deco buildings. The most ambitious attempts to realize it were made in studies for Rockefeller Center, but it did not appear in the complex as built.

A final ingredient of Art Deco is suggested by a restoration of King Solomon's Temple and Citadel which Helmle & Corbett drew up about 1925. A full-scale replica was to be built at the 1926 Sesquicentennial Exhibition in Philadelphia, where the public was to be able to rub elbows with employees dressed as ancient Israelites and later, having left the buildings, was to see them go up in simulated flames. This construction was apparently never built. Who was to have paid for it if it had been or what it was to have advertised, if anything, we are not told. The image is clear, though—an eye-boggling and exotic (yet educational) environment open to the public. The project strikes us as tawdry, but its character was to be an element in the Art Deco buildings to come. By a slight shift of locale it could evoke the images of Babel and Babylon that were associated with the New York skyscraper. Enough was thought of it for it to be published in *Pencil Points*;[21] it was sent to an exhibition of American work held in Berlin at the beginning of 1926; and Corbett lectured on it a year or two later.

In 1925 there was, quite apart from the Paris Exposition, increasing contact with the foreign architectural world, and the building boom began. The number of new office buildings built in 1925—fifteen—was not matched in any year after World War II till 1957. The number built in 1926, thirty, has not been matched since.[22] At the end of 1925 American architects put together an exhibition of their work and of America's architectural past for the Berlin Akademie der Künste.[23] In some respects this exhibition was made up of the sort of material that might be buried in a time capsule. It did, however, sum up what seemed significant in the work of the early twenties. Among New York efforts (which were selected by Harvey Wiley Corbett and Alfred Bossom [1881-1965], an English architect working in New York at the time) the show included the studies of the zoning envelope and of the multilevel traffic solution as well as of Solomon's Temple. In a selection of current New York buildings two were Art Deco, one virtually complete and the other a project. The first was McKenzie, Voorhees & Gmelin's Barclay-Vesey Building. The second was described as a "new building for an insurance company" by Buchman & Kahn. This was clearly their Insurance Center Building for 80 John Street.

Art Deco Beginnings

Construction of the Barclay-Vesey Building (1) had begun in 1923. Brickwork was started in 1924. In the summer of 1925 the editor of *The American Architect* wrote one of the architects, Stephen Voorhees (1878-1965, Princeton), that it was the finest modern building in America. It opened early in 1926 as an equipment and administrative center for the New York Tele-

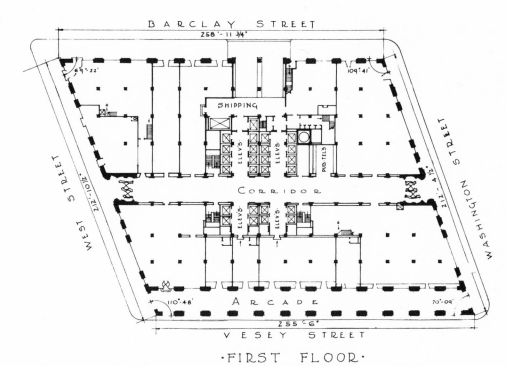

·FIRST FLOOR·

McKenzie, Voorhees & Gmelin, Barclay-Vesey Building, 1923-26, plan.

phone Company. The general form of the building had been determined by the zoning ordinance; its height was that at which the cost of space in the building met the market value of such space elsewhere in the city, a suitably hard-nosed criterion.[24] The tower of the building was on the model of Saarinen's Tribune entry and was treated with buttresses (1A). On the exterior of the building decoration in the form of fruit, animals, and human figures appears in low relief (1B). This ornament was said by some to be descriptive of the products formerly sold on the site, where there had been a produce market, and was also said to be "derived from marine sources, suggesting the proximity of the sea and maritime commerce."[25] The presence of aborigines and elephants among the fruit was not explained. Fruit continues on the lobby walls (1D). The elevator doors are demonstrably hand-crafted (1E). Lewis Mumford wrote that "the main hall . . . is as gaily lighted and decorated as a village street in a strawberry festival."[26]

At street level on the south side is an arcade within which the sidewalk passes (1C and plan) and onto which shops were intended to open. Because the Barclay-Vesey was some distance from other office buildings at the southern tip of Manhattan, this covered way seems never to have had much success as a shopping arcade. But it was built as a compromise solution to the city's plan

Buchman & Kahn, Insurance Center Building, 1926-27 (photograph of model).

to widen Vesey Street here,[27] and it seems to have been the first appearance of an element of the multilevel traffic plan.

The designer of the Barclay-Vesey Building, Ralph Walker (1889-1973, MIT), had clearly committed himself to most of this before the 1925 Exposition took place. But the executive floor may have been affected by that event. The anteroom there has a cornice which, though as foliate as the lobby below, in being faceted seems to derive from German Expressionist sources (1G). What this cornice may be is a first sign that, because of the 1925 show, modern styles were becoming acceptable. "Trivial reminiscences of the Gothic have fallen away," wrote Fiske Kimball, "puerile suggestions of historic style no longer mar the interior. As in the best German work, all is smelted anew in the creative spirit."[28] McKenzie, Voorhees & Gmelin should have been the more accessible to German ideas in that one partner, Paul Gmelin (1859-1937), was German born and trained. The boardroom is paneled. Between the panels decorative tree trunks seem to rise to a foliate cornice and to a similar grill above the door (1F). Today we are prepared to think of a boardroom as something of a jungle; evidently in the twenties its occupants, and Ralph Walker too, considered it something closer to Adam's hut in Paradise.

Construction on the second Art Deco building exhibited in Berlin, the Insurance Center Building, was not to start until March 1926. It was represented by a rendering, it seems, and by a photograph of a model. These show a clean-lined setback office building. Raised vertical lines at the setbacks help it to avoid successfully the appearance of a stack of boxes. What is not quite apparent, at least in the photograph of the model, is the character of the decoration towards the bottom of the building. A form of zigzag band occurs there which was repeated frequently in the Art Deco architecture to come (3). Like the cornice in the Barclay-Vesey anteroom, it may not have come directly from a particular building at the Paris Exposition; such forms can have been available from a number of sources. Ely Jacques Kahn, the architect of the building, wrote much later of the Furniture Exchange Building, built in 1926, that in designing its cornice he had "had in mind the texture of fabric."[29] But another possible source for such zigzags could have been the work of Adolfo Best-Maugard, a Mexican artist who had exhibited and lectured in New York and who brought out a book on design in 1923[30] (an English translation was published by Knopf in 1927[31]). Such designs as Best-Maugard's, if they were of in-

Buchman & Kahn, Furniture Exchange Building, 1926, detail.

fluence, would have had the appeal of being both primitive and modern.

In 1926 too forms that clearly had come from Paris appeared on the Lowell, an apartment house on East 63rd Street by Henry C. Churchill (1893-1962, Cornell) and Herbert Lippmann (b. 1889, Columbia). It exhibited a number of the characteristics of the Art Deco architecture that would develop. One was the quality of being almost a stage set carefully related to the street onto which the building faced. Others were the use of handicrafts and of color. The building, otherwise brick-clad, was faced on its ground-floor street front with glazed terra-cotta. The façade was in a modernized Classical form, in color, and for the most part in two dimensions. In only a few places, as in a form of pediment over the main doorway and in some pilasters, did it swell from the wall (4*). A contemporary reviewer wrote: "It is not by accident that the façade gives the momentary impression of being a back-drop, but rather an intentional declaration that the architects believe a façade can be more successfully painted, so to speak, on a building than modelled on one. . . ."[32] The façade is perhaps also characteristic in incorporating the entrance to a restaurant which the building contained, emphasizing the building's multiple purpose. The metalwork for the lamps at either side of the main doorway was done by Walter von Nessen; the mosaic above was designed by Bertram Hartman and executed by the Ravenna Mosaic Company. Gates had been made for the restaurant by Edgar Brandt and metal doors for the building by his New York company, Ferrobrandt. This was clearly a craft-oriented modernism. The year before, Ferrobrandt, under Jules Bouy, had made wrought-iron gates that could have come directly from Paris for the Cheney Brothers Silk Store designed by Howard Greenley (2A and B). Here a screen at the entrance to the building itself (the Madison-Belmont of Warren & Wetmore) was also done by Ferrobrandt (2C).

The Insurance Center, the Barclay-Vesey, and the Lowell suggest three courses which New York Art Deco architecture was to take. The first building had walls composed of woven patterns in terra-cotta; the firm of Buchman & Kahn, which designed the Insurance Center, put up a series of buildings with more explicitly woven forms in color in the following years. The second was a massive building with crag-like forms and brick walls which (to viewers of the time) were especially appropriate to the steel-framed building—they were "veneers of thin wall hung over skeleton frames";[33] the firm that designed the telephone company building made a house style of this type of volume hung with walls that became ever more explicitly hung in folds. The third was a building the facing of whose lower floors had the character of a stage set carefully related to the street.

Kahn and Others

Ely Jacques Kahn (1884-1972, Columbia, Ecole des Beaux-Arts) was the son of an Austrian-born importer of glass and mirrors; his elder sister Rena Rosenthal was, in the twenties, an importer of European arts and crafts. In 1915 Kahn joined a firm, previously Buchman & Fox, that had long specialized in commercial

* Buildings illustrated in the separate color section are marked with an asterisk in the list of buildings which starts on page 83.

buildings. By the middle twenties Kahn was doing a series of large, soundly designed[34] commercial buildings in the city, for which he had developed a vigorous, personal style of decoration. For a time in 1927 and 1928 they appear with woven forms in brightly colored terra-cotta on their walls. The masterpiece was his office building at the bottom of Park Avenue (6A). The color there, which appeared on the setbacks, was meant to be seen from the surrounding streets as the building's only exterior decoration. This colored terra-cotta was designed with the help of Leon Victor Solon (1872-?), an English-born artist and architectural writer. Solon had written on the colors used in classical antiquity;[35] and those on the Park Avenue Building were intended to reproduce the Greek primaries.[36] Its owners showed some qualms about this use of color on an exterior and, according to Kahn, Raymond Hood was brought in to reassure them that what was being proposed was good. Colored terra-cotta was also used on two other buildings, one on West 39th Street of 1927 (7) and the other at 261 Fifth Avenue of 1928-29 (21A). Eventually exterior color was used less by Kahn. However, he continued to use painted plaster, brass, and brightly colored mosaics in building lobbies whose lines suggest the headlong flow of the citizens of Gotham to and from their work (21B, 24). Kahn put up over thirty buildings in the seven years from 1925 to 1931.[37] Many were in the garment district south of Times Square (16, 80, 81). Some were in the printing district east of Grand Central Station, and some were insurance buildings northeast of Wall Street. One was for the film industry (24A and B). Only the Squibb Building (40) was what could be called a skyscraper. A reason for the consistent quality of Kahn's work, despite the variety of purposes for which these buildings were built, was that many of them were designed for two real estate promoters, Abe Abelson and Louis Adler,[38] who apparently recognized the soundness of the buildings Kahn was doing, while imposing few preconceptions on him as to what the appearance of buildings should be.

The firm of McKenzie, Voorhees & Gmelin, which after the completion of the Barclay-Vesey Building became Voorhees, Gmelin & Walker, also did a great many buildings for one client, the telephone company. They put up a series of buildings throughout the city in the late twenties, many with curtain-like brick walls and faceted lintels and copings (44, 45, 46). But their work was not confined to the telephone company. In 1928-30 they did a headquarters for Western Union with shaded orange

Joseph Urban, Ziegfeld
Theater, 1926-27.

brick walls (27A and B). The entrances to the Western Union
Building are in proscenium form and contain curtain-like screens
in glass and bronze. In 1929-30 Voorhees, Gmelin & Walker did
a headquarters for the Salvation Army (36A) incorporating an
office tower, a women's dormitory, and a temple, again in massive volumes hung with brick and stone in the manner of curtains. Within the theater-like temple (36B) the faceted ceiling

is cut out in willow patterns to overcome any illusion of weight. The walls of a building at the corner of Wall Street and Broadway built for Irving Trust in 1929-32 were even more explicitly curtain-like (54B and C). The interiors of a main banking room on the ground floor (54D) and of a lounge at the top of the building (54H) are faceted spaces. Such spaces seemed (to other architects as well as to Voorhees, Gmelin & Walker) the appropriate form for the destination of the hurrying citizens of the city.

The stage-set character of Art Deco buildings was demonstrated at its most explicit in the Ziegfeld Theater by the Austrian born and trained designer Joseph Urban (1872-1933). Urban, who was older than most of the New York Art Deco architects, had first come to this country in connection with the Austrian exhibit at the 1904 Louisiana Purchase Exposition in St. Louis and had returned to America to stay in 1911. By the twenties he had a reputation as a versatile designer of interiors and of stage sets for Boston and New York opera companies as well as for Ziegfeld productions. He showed an assurance in his designs that his younger colleagues lacked, and his buildings seem less enamored of a skyscraper formula than do others. His Ziegfeld Theater was striking in terms of our concern in having a façade in the form of a proscenium reflecting the real proscenium within (though not its particular form). This façade was described at the time as "a brilliant attempt to bring the stage in stone onto the street."[39]

Skyscrapers

In the twenties the archetypical modern American building was the skyscraper. The first real skyscraper to be started in the twenties was the Chanin Building of Sloan & Robertson begun in 1927.[40] (One of the last skyscrapers of the boom was to be the Empire State; the briefness of the period in which most of the Art Deco buildings were built is underlined by the fact that construction began on the Empire State six days after completion of the Chanin). As had been the case with the Barclay-Vesey and with the first skyscraper apartment building, the Panhellenic tower (see below), the Chanin's point of departure was Saarinen's Tribune entry (its top is to the left in color plate 57). It shared with other New York Art Deco buildings a carefully developed relationship to the street (9A and B), and its architects were clearly concerned that interiors have a popular and educative character rather than being simply useful. It also enjoyed a

William Van Alen, building on the northeast corner of Seventh Avenue and 33rd Street.

limited realization of the multilevel ideal. The lobby contained shops and restaurants; in the basement was a Baltimore and Ohio Railroad Motor Coach depot (accessible to buses by an entrance on the south side of the building).[41] From the basement too there was access to the Grand Central subway station. On the fiftieth floor, high above, there was a theater,[42] and above that an executive office level for the Chanin brothers, whose construction firm had put the building up, and an observation deck. The street level lobby in marble and brass was designed to offer the casual visitor as rich and eventful a welcome as would a movie palace of the period (9C, D, and E). The decorations in the lobby by René Chambellan (1893-1955) reportedly tell "symbolically . . . the story of a city in which it is possible for a man to rise from humble station to wealth and influence by the sheer power of his mind and hands"[43] (9C). A visitor to the Chanin organization was met by wrought-iron gates whose themes were energy, apparently, and machinery, art and money (9F). All of this was optimistic, instructive, and crafted—an impressive amenity accessible to the public.

From a hostile viewpoint the nadir of Art Deco design was probably the Chrysler Building. In 1928 announcement was made of the impending construction of a Reynolds Building designed by William Van Alen (1882-1954, Pratt, Paris Prize[44]). This was to be "surmounted by a glass dome, which, when lighted from within, will give the effect of a great jewelled sphere."[45] Before construction started, the lease on the site (from Cooper Union) and the plans were sold to Walter Chrysler. The plans were then somewhat modified—the building was lowered and its crowning motif changed. It was constructed in 1928-30. In the early years of the decade Van Alen had done a number of steel-framed buildings, many of them for Child's Restaurants, whose use of clearly nonstructural, though masonry, curtain walls and window frames set virtually at the surface of the wall was designed to express the nature of their construction.[46] In several store designs he had earned a reputation for doing the startling and dramatic thing.[47] If that was what was expected of him, his Chrysler did not disappoint. Proscenium-like entrances hold glass and metal screens lit from behind and decorated with fabric patterns (26H and I). Inside, within the triangular concourse (see plan), coved lighting over exits and elevator lobbies appears in the form of raised curtains (26J). "And as it is a commercial proposition, embodying the emblazonment of automotive progress," wrote the architect and critic Kenneth Murchison (1872-1938, Columbia, Ecole des Beaux-Arts) of the completed building, "why should the architect have hesitated a moment in being the Ziegfeld of his profession. . . ?"[48] In the basement there are shops, and connection was made with the IRT subway system, one which the subway company itself vigorously but unavailingly opposed. The exterior walls above the lowest floors have what was described at the time as the form of a basket-weave (26G).[49] Higher up, at the base of the tower, the building is pinched out at its corners (at a level which includes a decorative frieze of automobile hub caps and mudguards) in an attempt to overcome an optical illusion in which buildings that had horizontally banded towers seemed broader at their tops than at their bases[50] (26F). Within the crowning motif of the building was a luncheon club, whose main dining room had a German Expressionist character (26N). Still higher, above the club's gymnasia, there was originally an observation level, also Expressionist in character, where Walter Chrysler's original handmade tools (now in Detroit) were on display—again the educative touch.

The first apartment skyscraper was John Mead Howells' Panhellenic tower designed on the model of Saarinen's Tribune Tower project[51] and built off 49th Street near the East River in

William Van Alen, Chrysler Building, 1928-30, plan.

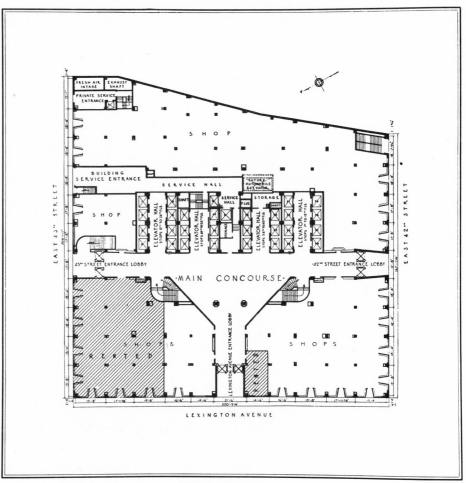

FIRST FLOOR PLAN

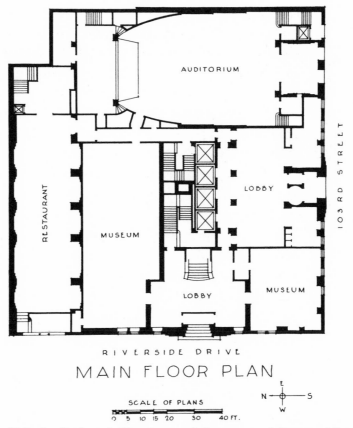

MAIN FLOOR PLAN

Helmle, Corbett & Harrison and Sugarman & Berger, Master Building,
1928-29, plan.

1927 (8). In 1928-29 a skyscraper apartment hotel was built on
Riverside Drive to designs of Helmle, Corbett & Harrison and
Sugarman & Berger (19A and B). It incorporated a museum for
the Russian painter and theatrical designer Nicholas Roerich,
studio space and an auditorium for the Master Institute of United
Arts, and a restaurant (see plan). The building struck its architects as remarkable because it used shaded brick, starting
with deep purple at the base of the building and rising to light
grey at the top.[52] This shading was an optical device, used on a
number of Art Deco buildings, which was said to make a building
look taller and to give a viewer the illusion of sunlight even on an
overcast day.[53] The Riverside Museum was designed to be artificially lit—such lighting was an innovation at the time. It also
seems remarkable now that the Master Institute included among
its faculty and lecturers Alfred Bossom, Claude Bragdon, Norman
Bel Geddes, Robert Edmund Jones, Lee Simonson, and Adolfo
Best-Maugard,[54] all of whom seem to have had significant though

Howells & Hood, 3 East 84th Street, 1928, rendered by Donald Douglas.

oblique impact on New York architectural design in the twenties.

From 1928 on there arose on Central Park West a series of large apartment houses, seven in all, which still make of that avenue a showplace for Art Deco. Of these the most interesting, in some ways, are the three designed by Schwartz & Gross (20, 64, 66), each with its distinctive ground-floor and crowning motifs. Throughout the late twenties and early thirties Art Deco was being applied too to an ever greater range of building types. In the Stewart & Company building of 1928-30 (25) designed by Warren & Wetmore (altered by Ely Kahn for Bonwit Teller) and in Starrett & Van Vleck's Bloomingdale's addition of 1930 (56) it was applied to the department store. A skyscraper garage was built in 1929-30, the Kent Columbus Circle Garage (43) by Jardine, Hill & Murdock; and there was a stock exchange façade in 1930, the Curb Exchange of Starrett & Van Vleck (59). Louis Allen Abramson and F. P. Platt & Brother designed a number of buildings for the Horn & Hardart chain of automated restaurants (29, 69, 70). There was also an Art Deco prison, the House of Detention for Women (55), 1929-32, by Sloan & Robertson, and an Art Deco church, the Fourth Church of Christ Scientist, 1931-32 (93), by Cherry & Matz.

Hood

An architect who built few buildings—some four Art Deco ones[55] —but who was as highly regarded as any New York architect of the twenties was Raymond Hood. In 1928 a small apartment house was put up to his designs on East 84th Street just off Fifth Avenue (14). On it appeared for the first time the recessed metal spandrels between vertical masonry strips (the spandrels derived ultimately from Sullivan's) that were to become a standard feature of many Art Deco skyscrapers. As this building was rendered for publication, it was represented as modern (an automobile is seen being unloaded in the foreground), but its stone facing is depicted as time-worn.[56] A desirable permanence seems thereby to have been suggested. Hood himself thought in longer time spans than we would consider practical. "The skyscraper problem is new," he wrote, "we have practically no traditions and, after all, serious architectural study is a new thing in this country; so it is fortunate that up to the present no one has formulated too strict a set of rules for our guidance. Another hundred years may, of course, change this. . . ."[57]

By designing the News Building of 1929-30 in a form ap-

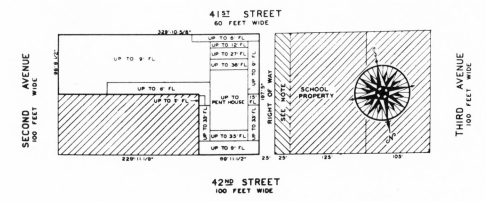

DIAGRAM OF AIR AND LIGHT CONDITIONS AT VARIOUS FLOORS

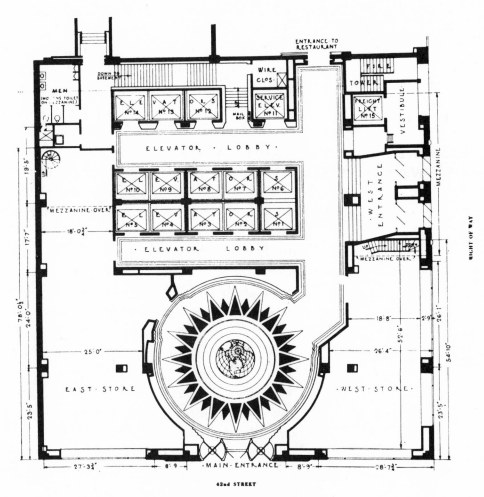

PLAN OF FIRST FLOOR

Howells & Hood, News Building, 1929-30, plans.

proaching that of a slab, Hood escaped the skyscraper formula of a prism with setbacks and a tower above. No sharp distinction was made between tower and base (35). Critics have considered this and Hood's McGraw-Hill Building (82) as International Style. But the News at its base is enriched with decorative bronze (35A and D). In its lobby (see plan) a globe revolves below a faceted ceiling of black glass (35F). The intention was in no way International Style. Hood's purpose in striping the exterior of the building (35B and C) was the same as his purpose in making his earlier American Radiator Building black—to hide the windows. "A wall that pretends to be a wall hates to be shot full of holes," as Edwin Avery Park paraphrased his thought.[58] In the McGraw-Hill Building of 1929-30 Hood turned to a machine aesthetic in the streamlined lobby and ground-floor exterior (82A). Yet his surfacing material for the building above was the colored craft material, terra-cotta, of the first Art Deco buildings.[59] Hood's final achievement was at Rockefeller Center, where it can be assumed that the slab of the RCA Building (90A) owes its form to Hood and to his News Building. It should be noted that at the Center the design is rationalized. Just as the crowning gesture of the Chrysler Building (26D) became transformed on the Empire State Building, 1930-31, of Shreve, Lamb & Harmon,[60] (76) to the symbolically functionalist form of a dirigible mooring mast, so the form of Hood's slab at Rockefeller Center follows function, as it were. All office space in the slab is to be no more than approximately twenty-seven feet from a window, and so the building is sculpted back as banks of elevators fall off.

The Center succeeds especially well at reaching some of the goals it shared with previous Art Deco buildings. The relation of the Fifth Avenue buildings of the Center, with the RCA Building behind them, to the avenue itself is especially successful (97, 102, 103). The Center, with its shops, arcades,[61] restaurants, theaters, skating rink, and tours, is accessible and popular as none of our postwar office buildings on their aloof plazas have, it is true, even aimed to be. Understandably, because of the length of time over which it was designed and built, the Center has one foot in the earlier craft-oriented Art Deco and another in the machine-oriented later phase. Though the Center retained the crafted metal spandrels of the earlier buildings (90C), it otherwise made an uncertain shift from the craft to the machine aesthetic. In the process, the work of artists who were employed to embellish the Center, work no longer satisfactorily a part of the architecture, became less than adequate as art standing on its own.

Much has been written about the process by which Rockefeller Center was designed by the group of architects involved: Benjamin Wistar Morris, Reinhard & Hofmeister, Corbett, Harrison & MacMurray, and Hood, Godley & Fouilhoux.[62] Arcades, elevated walkways, and pedestrian bridges played a part in a variety of early schemes, but they were lost in the Center as built. The individual architects, starting from scratch, as with a Beaux-Arts design problem, could devise radically varied designs for the Center.[63] But there is an inescapable similarity between the Center as eventually built and a major early solution by Benjamin Wistar Morris and Reinhard & Hofmeister at a time when the centerpiece of the whole was still to be a Metropolitan Opera House.[64] In both, a promenade splitting the central block leads to a plaza in front of the principal building. In collaboration, the architects—perhaps because collaboration in the first, crucial stage of design had not been part of their training—could at best only develop a solution already decided on, that is, develop another man's esquisse. A description of the Associated Architects' office procedure points only to efficiency at getting plans out as needed rather than to getting the best from each designer.[65] It is as though the Center were both the greatest achievement of Art Deco and the Waterloo of the Beaux-Arts architect.

Elsewhere Art Deco became in these years of the Depression the style of neighborhood movie house remodelings, of block after block of small apartment houses in the Bronx, and of government buildings like Cross & Cross's Federal Building (101). It was the style of the Kress's (106), Grant's and Woolworth's on New York's main street just as it was their style on the Main Streets of hundreds of other towns in a slump. In 1939, Harvey Wiley Corbett was at last able to realize his dream of Solomon's Temple when he designed New York's Criminal Courts Building, the Tombs (112). But by this time those who took their architecture seriously had long since turned their attention to the International Style.

Journalism

At its start New York Art Deco had a good press. Lewis Mumford said that the Barclay-Vesey Building (apart from its "strawberry festival" ornament) was "clear and logical, inflexibly committed to its programme."[66] Of Ely Kahn's Park Avenue Building he wrote, ". . . one building like this, which faces the entire problem of design, and has a clear unflinching answer for each question, may well serve to crystallize all the fumbling and uncertain elements in present-day architecture."[67] The building was written up in the *Architectural Record* by the very same Leon Solon who had had a hand in its design.[68] One cannot have a better press than that.

Yet the architectural journalism of the day was in some ways less than adequate for the architecture it served. American architectural magazines in the twenties were only beginning to unite pictures with words. They started the decade with entirely separate sections of text and plates, and during the twenties text and pictures never quite succeeded in coming together. Texts rarely referred precisely to photographs as illustrations of their arguments; there was certainly not the present-day custom of using descriptive captions and of writing in a text only what can be attested to by a picture. Worse, illustrations were sometimes assigned to an article mistakenly, as though, say, any modern buildings could illustrate any article on modern architecture.[69]

The journalism of Art Deco, as an architecture of "both-and," tended to be imprecise. There was no one good reason for doing something; a design might have several explanations, all acceptable. This did not hurt design, but it encouraged a journalism which was not incisive and adopted no particular critical stance. Art Deco and its journalism were a pushover for the International Style critics with their verbal attack and defense, their sloganeering, and their emphasis on simplification rather than ambiguity. They implied that the Art Deco architect had had International Style intentions but that his resolve had failed him. Henry-Russell Hitchcock, in the thirties one of the definitive spokesmen of the International Style, wrote in 1929 that the Stewart Store (25) was really quite good, but for the small amount of decoration on it. He doubted one could find a better building of comparable purpose in any European capital. He strongly recommended a view of the back of the building—"one of the finest bits of engineering architecture in New York"[70]— and, surprisingly, seemed to think the setbacks an indulgence of the architects. Douglas Haskell liked the Empire State Building, but he thought it had been at its best as a mere steel frame and had regressed when its curtain wall was added.[71]

For all the inadequacy of its journalism, the Art Deco was meant to be a consistent style. It was clearly not intended to be one of a number of styles which the architect might choose from, depending on the job and the client.[72] Even those who were hostile to it in the thirties understood this. Philip Johnson wrote that it had failed in its intention to be a style for two reasons:[73] that it had not had a consistent attitude to ornament, and that it had not lasted for ten years.[74] From our vantage point we can see that perhaps it did have a consistent attitude to ornament (though clearly to Johnson the only acceptable, consistent attitude would have been repudiation of it). As for those obligatory ten years, why, by the time the last buildings illustrated in this book were built, it had lasted ten years, and a little over.

Cervin Robinson

NOTES

1. An approving view of the skyscraper was expressed by Thomas E. Tallmadge in *The Story of Architecture in America* (New York: W. W. Norton, 1927), pp. 295-96.
2. American views hostile to the skyscraper appear in George C. Nimmons, "Skyscrapers in America," and in William Stanley Parker, "Skyscrapers Anywhere," both in *Journal of the American Institute of Architects*, 11 (Sept. 1923), 370-72. G. H. Edgell takes them to be inevitable in *The American Architecture of To-Day* (New York and London: Charles Scribner's Sons, 1928), pp. 358 and 362.
3. John F. Harbeson, *The Study of Architectural Design* (New York: Pencil Points Press, 1926), p. 127. This was the publication in book form of a series of articles which had appeared in *Pencil Points* over a period of years. The series had started in 2 (Jan. 1921), 19.
4. Throughout this text the school at which an architect studied is given after his dates. Where several names form the name of a firm, dates and schools are given in a footnote.
5. Raymond M. Hood, "Exterior Architecture of Office Buildings," *Architectural Forum*, 41 (Sept. 1924), 97.
6. Harbeson, p. 7.
7. Harbeson, p. 78.
8. Harbeson, p. 17.
9. It was also no doubt influenced by other even more progressive foreign entries to the same competition, which was published as *The International Competition for a New Administration Building for the Chicago Tribune, MCMXXII* (Chicago: The Tribune Company, 1923).
10. For the response to Saarinen's entry see Tallmadge, p. 290.
11. John Taylor Boyd, Jr., "The New York Zoning Resolution and its Influence upon Design," *Architectural Record*, 48 (Sept. 1920), 193-217; Harvey Wiley Corbett, "High Buildings on Narrow Streets," *American Architect*, 119 (8 June 1921), 603-8, 617-19; Aymar Embury II, "New York's New Architecture, the Effect of the Zoning Law on High Buildings," *Architectural Forum*, 35 (Oct. 1921), 119-24; Irving K. Pond, "Zoning and the Architecture of High Buildings," *Architectural Forum*, 35 (Oct. 1921), 131-34; Harvey Wiley Corbett, "The Influence of Zoning on New York's Skyline," *American Architect*, 123 (3 Jan. 1923), 1-4; Harvey Wiley Corbett, "Zoning and the Envelope of the Building," *Pencil Points*, 4 (April 1923), 15-18; and "Effect of New York Zoning Resolution on Commercial Buildings," *American Architect*, 125 (18 June 1924), 547-51.
12. Corbett, "Zoning and the Envelope of the Building."

13. Raymond Hood, "The American Radiator Company Building, New York," *American Architect*, 126 (19 Nov. 1924), 470.

14. See Kenneth M. Murchison, "The Chrysler Building as I See It," *American Architect*, 138 (Sept. 1930), 28 and 30.

15. Such an accepting attitude had a place in training too: Harbeson, pp. 71 and 72: ". . . having made a bad esquisse, . . . there is nevertheless a great value in carrying the problem through to a finish . . . the constant need for ingenuity to counteract the bad qualities of such an esquisse . . . is a real training for the problems of office work, where site, questions of construction, or the idiosyncrasies of a client frequently prevent an easy 'parti' and call for a display of ingenuity."

16. Edwin Avery Park, *New Backgrounds for a New Age* (New York: Harcourt Brace & Co., 1927), pp. 141-42.

17. See p. 61 of the Bletter essay, on Semper.

18. Paul T. Frankl, *New Dimensions: The Decorative Arts of Today in Words and Pictures* (New York: Payson & Clarke, 1928), p. 55.

19. Claude Bragdon, *The Frozen Fountain* (New York: Alfred A. Knopf, 1932), p. 11: "A building a fountain: how clarifying a point of view! . . . The needle-pointed *flèche* of the Chrysler tower catches the sunlight like a fountain's highest expiring jet."

20. Thomas Adams, *The Building of the City*, Regional Plan, Vol. II (New York: Regional Plan of New York and its Environs, 1931), p. 309.

21. "Dr. John Wesley Kelchner's Restoration of King Solomon's Temple and Citadel, Helmle & Corbett, Architects," *Pencil Points*, 6 (Nov. 1925), 69-86.

22. See Gordon D. MacDonald, *Office Building Construction, Manhattan 1901-1953* (New York: Real Estate Board of New York, 1952), and Samuel B. Ruckley, *Rebuilding Manhattan: A Study of New Office Construction* (New York: Real Estate Board of New York, 1972).

23. A catalog was published: *Ausstellung neuer amerikanischer Baukunst, Januar 1926*, Berlin, Im Verlage der Akademie der Künste zu Berlin.

24. The design of the building (apart from "elements contributing to the service of beauty") was explained in a manuscript of 1925, "A Big Building in New York," written by Stephen Voorhees for the "Princeton Engineering Journal" and in the possession of the New York Telephone Company. However, no "Princeton Engineering Journal" seems to have existed at the time.

25. Park, p. 150.

26. Lewis Mumford, "American Architecture Today," *Architecture*, 57 (April 1928), 185.

27. See "The Arcade," *Telephone Review* (Sept. 26, 1926), in possession of New York Telephone Company.

28. Fiske Kimball, *American Architecture* (Indianapolis and New York: Bobbs-Merrill, 1928), p. 216.

29. Ely Jacques Kahn, unpublished manuscript in the Avery Architectural Library, Chapter II, pp. 27-28.

30. Adolfo Best-Maugard, *Metodo de Dibujo, Tradición, Resurgimiento y Evolución del Arte Mexicano* (Mexico, Departmento Editorial de la Secretaría de Educación: 1923). As a student Best-Maugard had drawn up primitive designs for Franz Boaz. He had decided that all such primitive patterns could be reduced to a few elements and that by practicing such elements the person who was untrained in art could teach himself.

31. Adolfo Best-Maugard, *A Method for Creative Design* (New York and London: A. A. Knopf, 1927).

32. H. R. Shurtleff, "Apartment Hotel at 28 East 63rd Street," *Arts*, 11 (1927), 41.

33. Park, p. 151.

34. It is difficult some fifty years after the event to judge how well designed for its purpose a building may have been. We do know that Kahn was used repeatedly by a few clients to design a variety of specialized buildings. Despite the obvious care he gave to decoration, articles by Kahn rarely speak of it except in the most general terms. Instead, he tends to emphasize the need to satisfy the specialized needs of different clients. See Ely J. Kahn, "Economics of the Skyscraper," *Architectural Record*, 63 (April 1928), 298-301, and "Civilized Architecture," *Architectural Forum*, 52 (June 1930), 785.

35. Leon V. Solon, *Polychromy: Architectural and Structural, Theory and Practice* (New York, Architectural Record), 1924.

36. Kahn, unpublished manuscript, II. 4.

37. See *Ely Jacques Kahn*, Contemporary American Architects Series (New York: Whittlesey House, 1931), for illustrations of many Kahn buildings.

38. Kahn, unpublished manuscript, II. 7-11.

39. Tallmadge, p. 286.

40. John Sloan, 1888-1954, New York University; T. Markoe Robertson, 1868-1952, Yale, Ecole des Beaux-Arts. Though the Chanin was not intended to reach a record height, it had a greater number of stories than the Woolworth, the last building that had done so.

41. "B. O. Motor Coach Station, New York," *Architectural Forum*, 53 (Dec. 1930), 743, 744.

42. See R. W. Sexton, "A Theater on the Fiftieth Floor," *Architectural Forum*, 52 (May 1930), 727-30.

43. C. Adolph Glassgold, "The Decorative Arts," *Arts*, 15 (April 1929), 286.

44. The Paris Prize was awarded each year after a competition by the Society of Beaux-Arts Architects. The winner was sent, expenses paid, to the Ecole in Paris.

45. *American Architect*, 134 (Aug. 20, 1928), 269.

46. See Leon V. Solon, "The Passing of the Skyscraper Formula of Design," *Architectural Record*, 55 (Feb. 1924), 135-44, and Francis S. Swales, "Draftsmanship and Architecture, V, as Exemplified by the Work of William Van Alen," *Pencil Points*, 10 (Aug. 1929), 526.

47. Swales, 526.

48. Kenneth Murchison, "The Chrysler Building as I See It," p. 24.

49. Eugene Clute, "The Chrysler Building, New York," *Architectural Forum*, 53 (Oct. 1930), 403.

50. Clute, 404. Other buildings were given entasis, presumably to overcome this illusion: Urban's New School building, for instance, and, for that matter, the News, which shouldn't have had the problem.

51. It also clearly drew from Hood's American Radiator Building just as the latter had in part drawn from Corbett's Bush Terminal Building. But the primary liberating influence came from the Saarinen design.

52. Harvey Wiley Corbett, "Architecture of the Master Building," *Archer*, numbers 3 and 4 (1929), 26.

53. Henry S. Churchill, writing on "The State Tower Building in Syracuse," *Architectural Forum*, 50 (Jan. 1929), 1.

54. See announcements in issues of *Archer*, 1927-29.

55. This does not include his Rex Cole showrooms (of which one at least still stands in Bay Ridge as a Porsche-Audi salesroom).

56. "Aquatint Rendering by Donald Douglas," *Pencil Points*, 8 (Nov. 1927), 660. Douglas was a designer in Hood's office.

57. Raymond M. Hood, "Exterior Architecture of Office Buildings," *Architectural Forum*, 41 (Sept. 1924), 97.

58. Park, p. 149.

59. Not that terra-cotta was ever completely abandoned by Art Deco architects. A description of terra-cotta manufacture of the time can be found in W. A. Starrett, *Skyscrapers and the Men Who Build Them* (New York: C. Scribner's Sons, 1928), pp. 224, 235.

60. Richard H. Shreve, 1877-1946, Cornell; William Frederick Lamb, 1884-1952, Williams, Columbia, Ecole des Beaux-Arts; Arthur Loomis Harmon, 1878-1958, Chicago Art Institute, Columbia.

61. These are arcades, if passageways without arches but with shops can be described as shopping arcades.

62. Benjamin Wistar Morris, 1870-1944, Columbia, Ecole des Beaux-Arts; L. Andrew Reinhard, 1892-1964, Beaux-Arts Institute of Design; Henry Hofmeister 1890-1962, Beaux-Arts Institute of Design; Wallace K. Harrison, b. 1895, Ecole des Beaux-Arts; William H. MacMurray, 1868-1941; Frederick Augustus Godley, 1886-1961, Yale, MIT, Ecole des Beaux-Arts; Jacques André Fouilhoux, 1879-1945, Ecole Centrale des Arts et Manufactures. William H. Jordy, *American Buildings and Their Architects: The Impact of European Modernism in the Mid-Twentieth Century* (Garden City, N.Y.: Doubleday, 1972), p. 428, gives a useful summary of the literature on Rockefeller Center.

63. For Hood's, see Walter H. Kilham, Jr., *Raymond Hood, Architect—Form Through Function in the American Skyscraper* (New York: Architectural Book Publishing Co., 1973), p. 159. Plans of this Hood scheme and some others were published in Raymond Hood, "The Design of Rockefeller City," *Architectural Forum*, 56 (Jan. 1932), 1-7.

64. This was illustrated (Fig. 5) in Winston Weisman, "Who Designed Rockefeller Center?" *Journal of the Society of Architectural Historians*, 10 (March 1951), 14.

65. Wallace K. Harrison, "Drafting Room Practice," *Architectural Forum*, 56 (Jan. 1932), 77-80 and 81-84.

66. Lewis Mumford, "American Architecture Today," *Architecture*, 57 (April 1928) 185.

67. Mumford, 188.

68. Leon V. Solon, "The Park Avenue Building, New York City," *Architectural Record*, 63 (April 1928), 289-97.

69. Two examples of this casual attitude to illustration are: Samuel Chamberlain, "In Search of Modernism," *American Architect*, 131 (5 Jan. 1927), 71-74, and Talbot Faulkner Hamlin, "The International Style Lacks the Essence of Great Architecture," *American Architect*, 143 (Jan. 1933), 12-16. For that matter, in the Mumford article cited above a general view, identified as of the Park Avenue Building, one of the two buildings being discussed in the article, is in fact not a view of that building but of Kahn's Insurance Center Building.

70. Henry-Russell Hitchcock, "The Stewart Building," *Arts*, 16 (Oct. 1929), 124-27.

71. Douglas Haskell, "The Empire State Building," *Creative Art*, 8 (April 1931), 242-44.

72. This seems to have been true for whole buildings but not necessarily for every interior in them. The executive floor of Hood's McGraw-Hill Building was not Art Deco; and in the Cloud Club in the Chrysler Building only the main dining room was in the style.

73. Philip Johnson, "The Skyscraper School of Modern Architecture," *Arts*, 17 (May 1931), 575.

74. What he said precisely was that "a style must be worthy of continuing at least a decade."

J. M. van der Meij, Scheepvaarthuis, Amsterdam, 1912-16.

THE ART DECO STYLE

"Some of this modern mess you have created and never stop to analyze is really beautiful."

Artist addressing the public in Edwin Avery Park's
New Backgrounds for a New Age, 1927

Definition

In 1927, in *New Backgrounds for a New Age,* Edwin Avery Park insisted that a new age had dawned and should be expressed in art and architecture. He found that art was proclaiming our civilization, but to his dismay architecture and interior design seemed to be lagging behind. Describing the cultural milieu of the designer, for example, he wrote: "He will dance and dine to jazz, read 'Ulysses,' have himself psychoanalyzed, listen to Debussy, appreciate Cézanne, and ride in an aeroplane. But he will be installing an Empire suite in some wealthy lady's apartment. We have nothing to say for ourselves."[1]

This was written just as American architects were beginning to come to grips with the jazz age. Barely three years after Park's statement, a series of distinctive Art Deco skyscrapers altered the New York skyline, and hundreds of Art Deco shops, restaurants, and building lobbies exuded the spirit of modernity. The cityscape and its public interiors had changed, and the change could be seen by both the tourist and the office worker.

What made Art Deco buildings unique? What are the characteristics that differentiate them from architecture done in a Neogothic or Neoclassical manner? Did Art Deco in fact develop an idiom that would justify our calling it a style? The strength of the Beaux-Arts tradition in New York, still alive in the early twenties, would lead one to suspect that most architects, from the outset, were not interested in an overtly revolutionary style or a total break with the past, but more in a rephrasing of given modes.

Art Deco architecture depends first of all on a traditional form of an American commercial style: the skyscraper as it had evolved from its beginnings in Chicago in the late nineteenth century. No structural innovations or drastic changes in interior subdivision of spaces were introduced (except perhaps that internal walls were now often used as mere partitions to provide flexibility for office floors).[2] Louis Sullivan's precepts, stated in "The Tall Office Building Artistically Considered" of 1896, apply to most Art Deco skyscrapers as well. There is a ground floor with shops, banks, and other services amply spaced and with a "main entrance that attracts the eye to its location"; the exterior of the ground floor is treated in a "liberal, expansive, sumptuous way." The office floors are expressed uniformly; Sullivan had said to "make them look alike because they are all alike." The attic is dealt with emphatically to show that "the series of office tiers has come definitely to an end."[3] This basic three-part division was maintained in most Art Deco skyscrapers, with some minor additions. First, the multi-functional treatment of the ground floor, taken for granted by Sullivan, in many Art Deco buildings is expanded to include a more complex traffic circulation: access to subways, bus stops, and parking garages is now often incorporated into the planning of the lower section of a structure. Second, the zoning law affected the massing of tall buildings. In place of Sullivan's overhanging cornice, there appear a variety of stepped-back shapes, which are, when seen from afar, actually more distinctive as terminating points than Sullivan's flat roofs. There were, to be sure, later variations in the way architects dealt with the setback requirements, such as the less conventional arrangement of the building mass in the Daily News Building, or the gradual system of setbacks in the building group of Rockefeller Center, beginning with the low elevation of the structures along Fifth Avenue; the full height of the RCA Building is not achieved abruptly. By the time Rockefeller Center was designed, the idea of the tall building as a single slab had been changed by an approach to massing which kept the building more within human scale at its street façade or at least more within scale of the older urban fabric.[4] Naturally, these later projects were also larger than any that had been executed before, and the effect of their scale must have been an important concern of their architects.

Sullivan had also believed that the chief characteristic of the tall office building was its loftiness. This he described as its "dominant chord. . . . It must be tall, every inch of it tall. The force and power of altitude must be in it, the glory and pride of exaltation must be in it. It must be every inch a proud and soaring thing. . . ."[5] Indeed, in Sullivan's own tall buildings this is usually expressed by piers which rise uninterruptedly from the second floor to the attic level with recessed spandrels and windows. Precisely this effect is sought after in most Art Deco skyscrapers; whether the piers are classicizing and heavily articulated, or Gothicizing, more slender, and triangular, they almost always form the dominant vertical feature.

The most obvious element of Art Deco architecture is its use of sumptuous ornament, and the lush textures and color achieved by combining several materials, such as stone, brick, terra-cotta, and metal. Again, there is an aspect of this which can be tied to nineteenth-century architecture. Concentration of dynamic ornament around entrances and at the attic zone, with more structured ornamental patterns in spandrels, is also a feature of Sullivan's tall buildings and can be found with variations in Art Deco skyscrapers.

Color and ornament had, of course, been used extensively in Victorian architecture. John Ruskin in *The Stones of Venice* (1851-53) treats ornament in a way that is comparable to its use in Art Deco architecture—its primary justification is to delight. He wanted an ornament that was visually and sometimes even physically accessible. A similar obviousness and palpability resides in Art Deco decoration, as it does in any populist expression. As to the relation between ornament and structure, Ruskin was for an expression of structure, but not for an engineering aesthetic. He believed that ornament should not conceal construction, but neither should construction be revealed blatantly:

. . . it may sometimes, on the one hand, be necessary to conceal [the masonry] as far as may be, by delicate and close fitting, when the joints would interfere with lines of sculpture or of mouldings; and it may often, on the other hand, be delightful to show it, as it is delightful in places to show the anatomy even of the most delicate human frame: but *studiously* to conceal it is the error of vulgar painters, who are afraid to show that their figures have bones; and studiously to display it is the error of the base pupils of Michael Angelo, who turned heroes' limbs into surgeons' diagrams. . . .[6]

Ruskin saw the nonstructural wall areas between piers as a "wall veil," much as the twentieth-century architect would use the term "curtain wall." Instead of using the International Style's general mode of revealing structure by means of a glazed curtain wall, Art Deco architects "express" structure in Ruskin's sense in their opaque curtain walls.

At the same time it must be pointed out that color used in Art

Deco buildings does not always rely on the natural color of materials, as Ruskin had also recommended. Glazed tiles and polychrome terra-cottas are often used, in bright, vibrant, and startling colors. Sometimes whole buildings are shaded, beginning with a dark-toned brick at ground level and shading into lighter and lighter tonalities toward the top. Harvey Wiley Corbett's Master Institute and Riverside Museum (19), for example, changes from a dark purple below to a greyish color at the top; a similar effect is achieved in Schwartz & Gross' apartment house at Central Park West and 66th Street (64A). In other instances, large, bold ornament is used near the building's top, as in Kahn's office building at 2 Park Avenue (6A). The scale of this daring, vivid design was consciously geared to perception from a distance (Ruskin had also insisted that ornament remain readable from various vantage points).[7] A small-scale design in muted colors would have virtually disappeared from several blocks away. Thus, the Art Deco architect was not only concerned with giving the passerby and office worker an elevating experience by enhancing entrance area and lobby space with a profusion of ornament. He was equally concerned with having the building remain readable from a distance and with its general effect in the skyline, and therefore used unusual terminations at the top and ornament scaled to distance, effects that are today perhaps no longer as readily apparent, with the occlusion of so many Art Deco skyscrapers by later, taller buildings.

A similarity between nineteenth-century theory and contemporary developments was noted by Talbot Hamlin in an essay of 1932, "Is Originality Leading Us Into a New Victorianism?" He believed that behind the search for originality which he saw in all twentieth-century styles lay a theory of expressionism formulated by Ruskin and the French architectural theorist, Viollet-le-Duc. Despite the continued validity of nineteenth-century ideas, Hamlin found in contemporary architecture the same ferment of taste that had troubled the Victorians. He saw as the chief causes of a degradation of taste the following:

1. The commercialization of the search for originality in order to make new markets for new manufactured goods. This led inevitably to the fact that manufacturers and builders made things and houses to satisfy the masses, who are always the least educated, the least cultured parts of the population.
2. An innate love of richness and decoration on the part of the buying public that results so easily in excess and complexity.
3. A cultural condition, showing in politics, literature, and religion, of unprecedented hypocrisy, arrogance, distortion of values, and dishonesty.
4. The endless facility of the human mind in rationalization, that enables it to apply almost any given theory to almost any given facts.[8]

Ely Jacques Kahn as early as 1929 had similarly criticized the facile rush to novel forms: "The essential is honesty; the danger is the belief that freedom suggests acceptance of anything which is merely different. As any period has discovered there is always a great volume of freak, shoddy work being produced that cannot be avoided. Just now the tendency to jumbled, explosive geometric forms has led some designers to eccentricities that will quite as promptly be cast aside."[9]

These are in fact the problems any post-aristocratic architecture must face, problems that not only developed because of the rise of a nouveau riche class, but that are a deeper and an intrinsic part of the question of taste in a mass society, where style is no longer decreed from above by an aristocratic class. The attempts of the nineteenth-century design reformers notwithstanding, no one in modern society, not even the architect or artist, seems to have proper standing to legislate taste.

The design of architectural ornament is commonly the first indication of whether a building is Art Deco. It is in the specific arrangement of patterns that Art Deco is most directly indebted to the Paris 1925 Exposition Internationale des Arts Décoratifs et Industriels Modernes. However, some caution is called for, since the 1925 exhibition was itself already highly eclectic, and it is often quite difficult to tell whether a pattern should be classified as Cubist or Expressionist. In any case, many of the ornamental terra-cotta panels, spandrels, or metal screens of Art Deco architecture have the stylized floral patterns (2B, 9B, 70) and strident geometrics combining harsh angular forms with sections of circles and other softly curving shapes that are familiar from Art Deco crafts (9D, 9E, 26L).

Another of the more novel aspects of the style is the use of faceted, crystalline forms leading to an entrance, like a modern version of a Gothic splayed doorway (44, 46, 89). Sometimes faceting occurs at the ceiling, as in lobbies and lounges (35, 36), or, most visibly, in the crowning features of a building (54, 80). The source of this type of detailing appears to be German Expressionist architecture. Such sculptural effects were more typical of the earlier, arts-and-crafts oriented and Gothicizing aspect of the style. By the thirties one can also find more Constructivist effects, as in the top of the McGraw-Hill Building (82) or the Century and Majestic apartments (87, 96). But, as with many of the features of Art Deco architecture, one is not entirely certain that these forms are in fact Constructivist, for such interpenetrating forms could just as readily be traced to Frank Lloyd Wright.

Art Deco is, then, basically an eclectic style that makes simple definitions difficult. Most important, the style should not be defined solely in terms of its newer aspects—such as its ornament, streamlined forms, etc.—but must be seen together with its conservative elements—the older, commercial skyscraper architecture of which it is a continuation and the Beaux-Arts background of many of the Art Deco architects. All these characteristics coalesce in Art Deco architecture in a new way.

Art Deco architecture in New York was created mostly for big business. Yet the result was not an austere corporate imagery, but an architecture that was good advertising, meant to entertain and draw in the public. Together with Neoclassical features and the dry repetitiveness of commercial floors, there is also the Romantic interest in sensory experience through texture, color, and decoration. The Art Deco architect was not interested in the dematerialized ascetic expression of the International Style. Even when he conceived of his walls as "curtain-walls," they have the look of masonry walls, of traditional construction, with down-to-earth tactile effects. The passerby is supposed to empathize with the building as if it were some obvious, theatrical gesture taken from a Baroque painting. Such buildings are enticing on a common level like the ruddy cheeks of a Rubens Madonna. Mysteries of volume, ambiguities of transparent space, and forms hovering heavenward—subtleties found in International Style architecture—are absent from Art Deco design, which often attempts to provide the kind of style and elegance the contemporary public was more likely to have encountered in the theater or in films than in real life. Sometimes such attempts misfired and looked shrill. But the more successful ventures are examples of a decent pluralistic architecture.

Such conclusions, while based on Art Deco architecture in New York, represent general principles of the style. For example, Forrest F. Lisle, discussing Chicago's Century of Progress Exposition of 1933, writes in a similar vein:

Contrary to most historical and critical assessments of American architecture of the 1930's, Moderne architecture [his term for Art Deco] can be shown to have been the logical and thus, perhaps, "proper" stylistic choice, for America to have made in view of the nation's institutions, traditions, and ideals . . . it is demonstrable that basic to the development and acceptance of the Moderne was the existence of, and regard for, democratic, egalitarian, middle-class, commercial, free-enterprise, popular culture values and comprehensions.[10]

The sources of the Art Deco style of the Century of Progress fair he describes as follows:

4. THE LOWELL

Henry S. Churchill and Herbert Lippmann faced the ground floor of this steel-framed apartment house with glazed terra-cotta. Build in 1926 between Park and Madison on 63rd Street, the building incorporated a French restaurant, the Passy, which is still in business there. The mosaic above the entrance was designed by Bertram Hartman. Octagonal decorative panels were popularized by the Paris Exposition des Arts Décoratifs et Industriels of 1925 but had been used earlier by Secession designers.

6. THE PARK AVENUE BUILDING

A. The glazed terra-cotta at the top of this 1927 building by Ely Jacques Kahn was intended to reproduce the primary colors of Greek antiquity. The building is seen here with the Empire State Building (76) behind.

7. 42 WEST 39TH STREET

Buchman & Kahn built a second building in 1927, this one in the garment district and with glazed terra-cotta towards its base. The use of sumptuous and colorful ornament and the juxtaposition of a variety of materials is apparent here as in Kahn's Park Avenue building.

24. FILM CENTER BUILDING

A. The forms in the elevator lobby of this building of 1928-29 by Ely Kahn derive from fabric design. But their effect is to suggest the flow of the citizens of Gotham on their way to and from work. Horizontal striping, such as appears here, had been popularized by the 1925 Paris Exposition, but, like so much else of the Art Deco, had been used earlier by Viennese designers.

26. CHRYSLER BUILDING

B and C. The elevator doors and interiors of the cabs feature veneers of a variety of woods. The cabs came in four patterns, one of which is illustrated here.

35. THE NEWS BUILDING

A. Raymond Hood's building of 1929-30 is clad in alternating strips of white and red: white brick verticals—and windows with red shades below recessed spandrels of red and black brick.

This apartment building a few blocks south of Grand Central Station was designed by Bowden & Russell and built in 1930. Bright scales of color in terra-cotta appear on the tower of the building. The Chanin (9) and the Chrysler Building (26) are to the left beyond it.

57. THE TOWN HOUSE

64. CENTRAL PARK WEST AT 66TH STREET

A. Schwartz & Gross's apartment house of 1930 was one of a number of Art Deco buildings that had curtain walls of brick which shaded from a dark color at the base of the building to a light one at the top. The building was thereby to seem taller and to give the impression of being sunlit even on an overcast day.

60. TWENTIETH-CENTURY FOX BUILDING

A. A stained-glass window was set between the vestibule and lobby of the New York headquarters of a Hollywood movie company.

This building by Louis Allen Abramson is on 181st Street not far above the George Washington Bridge. Decorative bands appear on its stone-surfaced façade. The top band is in glazed terra-cotta. The lower, broader one is finished in metallic surfaces.

70. HORN & HARDART

82. McGRAW-HILL BUILDING

A. The streamlined entrance to this building of 1930-31 by Raymond Hood marks it as a late Art Deco building, but in its use of color it suggests the earlier craft phase of the style. An address sign originally set below the company's name is missing.

. . . the Paris 1925 Fair, Frank Lloyd Wright, cubism, machine ethics, Mayan forms, Pueblo patterns, Dudok, the Viennese Secession, modern interiors, the zoning-law setback. This large number of weakly related sources, readily identified as underlying the Moderne in America, begins to suggest the loose, broad, inclusive, less intense, rather indiscriminate, thus democratic, perimeters of the modern movement *here* as opposed to the impersonal, reductive, exclusive, more idealistic, more moralistic thrust of avant-garde Europe at this time.[11]

Despite the recent flurry of publications on Art Deco art, there has been to date no general book on the architecture of that period.[12] Those books on Art Deco art that do mention buildings do so peripherally and are often quite misleading: while earlier historians had neglected Art Deco in favor of the International Style, several authors of contemporary Art Deco books go now to another extreme and suggest that everything produced in the twenties and thirties is Art Deco, including International Style architecture.[13] The reader is never told exactly how someone like Corbusier, Gropius, or Mies is supposed to fit into the Art Deco style. We will have a more workable model of the styles of the twenties and thirties if we assume that there was an esoteric style, that is, the International Style, alongside of which developed a more popular style which has been named variously Art Deco, Modernistic, Jazz Modern, Zigzag Modern, Style 1925, the Twenties Style, the Thirties Style, Streamlined Modern, etc.[14] The most commonly used term at the moment is Art Deco (and so we have chosen to use it, despite its obvious inadequacies with respect to architecture because originally it implied only the decorative arts), a name that is based on the 1925 Paris Exposition Internationale des Arts Décoratifs et Industriels Modernes. In its own day this style was referred to in America, after some initial vacillations between "modernist" and "modernistic," as Modernistic from about 1928 onward.[15]

One of the major reasons why Art Deco has not previously become a standard chapter in architectural histories is that it was never as revolutionary as the International Style—some traditions were broken by the Art Deco architect but others were left intact. Its promoters did not want to upset the viewer—they wanted to find an *acceptable* modern style; one could call the Art Deco architect an avant-garde traditionalist. And while the architectural results were on occasion vulgar, the intention was to create a mass modern. In place of the undecorated, glazed, stuccoed, and severe façades of the International Style, the Art Deco architect provided rich textures, architectural ornament, and polychrome effects, a clear bridge to the architecture of the past.

Art Deco never looks intellectual and cool like the International Style, but is instead lavish and opulent, qualities that have a direct appeal to the senses. The style became acceptable to middle-of-the-road patrons of commercial architecture, many of whom seemed to have few convictions about architectural expression. Most of these real estate developers gave their architects free rein, as long as the style was new without being shocking. Art Deco became the style of such smart stores as Bonwit's, Bloomingdale's, and Tiffany's, it became the corporate style for the New York Telephone Company, of the elegant Waldorf-Astoria Hotel, of the garment district, of the Horn & Hardart automated restaurant chain, and of the movie palaces where officer workers and café society mingled.

Because Art Deco occupies a position somewhere between a "high" and a vernacular style—although a mass style, it was urbane and never possessed the naïveté of a folk style—its forms did not often spring from native creativity. It borrows from here and there and deserves a prize for eclecticism, a feature which has made it most elusive to analyze. Given its popular, eclectic nature, we should expect a long list of variables and sources, to which we will turn shortly.

Whether or not Art Deco became an American style—a phase that differs from European Art Deco—there are regional differences apparent to even a casual visitor to, say, Los Angeles or Philadelphia. In Los Angeles Art Deco was more strongly affected by the Mission style, by a precocious car culture, and by Hollywood.[16] In California, also, the building types in the style are more varied, and Art Deco does not remain as much restricted to high-rise buildings as elsewhere. Philadelphia's Art Deco is closer to that of New York City but often has a more forcefully expressed ornament. In fact, speculating on a modern style to come, an editor of *The American Architect* thought that any new styles of the future would not be national at all but regional.[17] It is conceivable, however, that there is a national style with regional variations. We present the New York Art Deco buildings as specific examples within this wider context.

If we rely for dating Art Deco on its varied terminology, we must assume that the Twenties Style, for instance, began in 1920 and ended in 1929. Of course, historical development is not that obliging. Another name, the "Style 1925," is much more specific, perhaps too precise. This appellation derives from the central event of the period, the Paris 1925 exposition. However, it is obvious that the style did not spring full-fledged into existence when the gates to the exposition opened, nor did it end suddenly when the exposition closed. Most authors on Art Deco crafts are agreed on 1925 as a pivotal and crucial date: they see the exhibition as both the climax and the popularization of the style and hence the beginning of its eclipse.[18]

For New York Art Deco architecture the conventional dating must be revised. Art Deco was not used here extensively until after the impact of the 1925 Paris exposition was felt. To be sure, a few early examples were erected between 1923 and 1927, but the style attained its greatest popularity between 1928 and 1931. There are in addition some structures that were begun in the late thirties. In any case, if we want to identify a high point of this popular style, it must be placed in the late twenties and early thirties. This is considerably later than the peak in arts and crafts; in part because architecture, being tied to a multitude of economic requirements, usually responds to a new style more slowly than the other arts, and in part because architectural training in New York had remained close to the Beaux-Arts tradition and its conservative method of education.

Alfred H. Barr, in the catalogue of the Museum of Modern Art's *Modern Architecture—International Exhibition* of 1932, sees Art Deco architecture clearly as a style, but as a style not worthy of the Museum of Modern Art. He finds that the Paris 1925 exposition had had more disturbing effects than the Chicago Tribune Tower competition of 1922:

Only recently has the deluge of modernistic decoration from Vienna, Paris, Stockholm, and Amsterdam begun to diminish, but not before our more advanced architects, already stimulated by Saarinen's success, had accepted the modernistic mode with enthusiasm and ornamented their buildings with zigzags and chevrons instead of Gothic crockets and Classical moldings. The modernistic style has become merely another way of decorating surfaces.[19]

Barr goes on to say that he hopes for a "genuine" new style, a style which will eliminate the confusion of the past, a style that will use light surfaces, open plans, a style that will emphasize volume over mass, and that will be without ornament—all clearly International Style principles. There are two significant points in Barr's statement. First, he calls the Art Deco architects "advanced" even though he does not approve of their style, indicating that the Art Deco architect was neither conservative enough to be dismissed outright by the Museum of Modern Art, nor, on the other hand, avant-garde enough to be in the museum's good graces. Further, it is interesting that Barr, while correctly identifying the eclecticism of Art Deco architecture, mentions only the newer European sources and fails to point out the older American precedents for the style. Of course, it must be remembered that he was writing at a time when the avant-garde insisted on a revolutionary credo and regarded the past as a confusing or irrelevant factor. In any case, let us now examine more specifically the European influences Barr mentions.

The French Influence

If we want to explore the multifarious sources for Art Deco architecture, it is best to begin with the 1925 Paris exposition, which in itself epitomized the style's characteristic quality of pastiche. To understand why the style of the 1925 exposition was not entirely novel, but was rather made up of novelties, we must first clarify the reason for the exhibition. In 1910 at the Paris Salon d'Automne an exhibition of German crafts had been held which met with great popular success (crowds had to be controlled by the police) and also made French artists and artisans realize that French production had not kept pace with the German arts and crafts development.[20] As early as 1907 the German Werkbund had been founded for the furtherance of the relation between architects, artists, craftsmen, and industry.[21] In France, on the other hand, design at the time was fairly conservative. This "design gap" was seen as an economic and competitive disadvantage, and to overcome it, plans were made, beginning in 1912, for an exhibition to be held in 1915 in Paris that would be an answer to Germany's dominance in the design field.[22] World War I interrupted the original plan. In 1922 it was resurrected, but the exhibition did not take place until 1925. By this time Germany was no longer just a competitor in the production of modern design; it was a conquered enemy nation, and what had originally been intended as an economic contest took on political overtones. The exhibition was ostensibly international, but Germany was invited too late for adequate organization and preparation and it declined. Thus Germany, the original cause of this design contest, was excluded, and the comparative merit of French and German design could not be evaluated at all. The political implications of the exposition are even clearer when the general layout of the site is examined: the main intersection at the exhibition grounds was reserved for the major nations allied with France during World War I—Britain, Belgium, Italy, and the United States.[23] The scheme was not carried out completely as planned only because the United States declined participation. Herbert Hoover, then Secretary of Commerce, wrote that America could not take part because no modern design was being produced there.[24] If Hoover's response seems odd, it can be partly understood in the light of the equally odd participation requirements set up by the exposition committee. Any works submitted were supposed to possess new inspiration and real originality, and any imitations of ancient styles were "strictly prohibited."[25] The understandable result of such a bureaucratic approach to new creation and disregard for normal stylistic development was that most of the works submitted frenetically displayed their novelty. It was modernity by official decree: let there be a new style.

On the other hand, this eagerness to be modern contrasts curiously with an equal reluctance to include examples of the revolutionary architecture of that period, especially the International Style. The products of the Bauhaus were not shown because they were German, but what is the explanation for the absence of

L. H. Boileau, Pavilion of the Bon Marché department store at the 1925 Paris show.

J. Hiriard, Tribout & Beau,
Pavilion of the Galeries
Lafayette, 1925 Paris show.

de Stijl design? And why did Corbusier have to occupy by night
a peripheral site for his *L'Esprit Nouveau* pavilion after having
been tipped off that it would be given to another entrant?[26] Why
did the commissioners have a six-foot palisade fence erected
around his pavilion obscuring it from view?[27] Together with
Melnikov's pavilion for the Soviet Union, Corbusier's pavilion
was the most avant-garde work of architecture of the whole exhibition. The reason for this reluctance was, it seems, that really
revolutionary forms were not sought—only a popularized image
of a modern style.[28]

This becomes especially clear when we consider that the demand for newness does not seem to have extended to the architecture of the exhibition itself. While most of the buildings have
the rich ornamental reliefs and decorative screens typical of Art
Deco, the architectural grouping and massing is, almost without exception, Neoclassical in spirit. The buildings are most
commonly based on centralized plans, or they exhibit bilat-
eral symmetry, with flanking wings and stepped roofs that as-
cend to a crowning pinnacle. In fact, one of the major entrances,
from the Place de la Concorde, is, with its forest of pylons,
strangely reminiscent of a National Socialist or Fascist scheme.
Thus, the architecture itself was quite conservative, and any
newness was carried by the surface ornament. It is in the decorative surfaces of this architecture that the "style" and the motifs
characteristic of Parisian Art Deco have all been brought together: stylized fountains, zigzag borders, and dense floral fields

packed into octagons, into spandrels, and into other geometric forms. There were some exceptions: both the Danish pavilion by Kay Fisker and the Dutch pavilion by J. F. Staal had a rich texture produced not through decorative panels but through an intricately organized pattern of exposed bricks, the latter in the manner of the Expressionist Amsterdam School. Further, Josef Hoffmann's Austrian pavilion, with its horizontally articulated bandings that were integrated with the structure, was austere in the context of the other pavilions.[29] In the courtyard of the Austrian pavilion was the only German design of the exposition, a "greenhouse" by Peter Behrens done in German Expressionist fashion with faceted, crystalline glass sections. Behrens' pavilion was there only because he had been invited by Hoffmann to participate in the Austrian entry (Behrens was teaching in Vienna at the time). Ely Jacques Kahn writing of the electrifying effect the 1925 Paris exposition had on him, singles out the Austrian and "German" pavilion as especially striking.[30]

Thousands of visitors from the United States came to the 1925 Paris exposition.[31] And just as France had been stimulated by the German exhibition of 1910, so the United States was inspired by this one. Although Hoover had not sent American representatives to the show, it was apparently not because he thought the exhibition unimportant but because he seems to have been truly convinced that the United States could not have come up with original designs. Even before the opening of the Paris exposition, he appointed a commission to visit Paris and write up a report for the benefit of American manufacturers. The commission in turn invited trade associations to appoint delegates, so that in the summer of 1925 eighty-seven delegates from such organizations as the American Institute of Architects, the Architectural League of New York, the Furniture Designers' Association, the American Construction Council, the Association of National Advertisers, the Society of Arts and Crafts, the Society of Interior Decorators, the New York State Department of Education, the Illuminating Engineering Society, the Silk Association of America, and United Women's Wear, as well as delegates from the Metropolitan Museum and from the New York Times, visited the exposition.[32] On their return the delegates made reports to their respective trade associations and published articles in trade papers on the exposition. The commission seems to have been completely taken in by the image France had wanted to convey ever since the successful German show of 1910. In a general report, one of the commissioners writes that German manufacture had been important because of the Werkbund until 1914, but that since the war—and here he quotes from a French writer—"France has taken a leaf from Germany's book."[33] The French intention to regain dominance in design met with complete success—commercial success, that is. Most visitors, like the American commissioners, did not inquire into the origins of the new styles presented at the exposition and naturally assumed that they were French. The show was so successful that to this day, several historians of the Art Deco style treat it as a primarily French phenomenon, rather than the eclectic one it was.

From the visual and written evidence one must conclude that it was the general impact of the Paris exposition—not individual French architects such as Robert Mallet-Stevens, André Lurçat, or Pierre Chareau—that affected American architects the most. The style of the exposition was further popularized in New York City by an exhibition of modern French furniture at Lord and Taylor's in 1928. Organized by Ely Jacques Kahn, the show included ensembles by such designers as Chareau, Ruhlmann, Jourdain, and Sue et Mare.[34] Henry-Russell Hitchcock commented in 1928 that within a year of the Paris exposition Art Deco products had been introduced to New York, although through commercial channels "rather than through architects and decorators."[35] Then in 1929, when zigzags were already flooding the market, the Metropolitan Museum held an exposition organized by Richard Bach, a curator of industrial arts and one of Herbert Hoover's commissioners for the Paris 1925 exposition. The Metropolitan show was an exhibition of contemporary American design called "The Architect and the Industrial Arts." Apparently because no American interior furnishings were available in the new style, most were designed by the architects themselves, including, among others, Raymond Hood, Ely Jacques Kahn, Ralph T. Walker, Joseph Urban, Eugene Schoen—all New York architects —John Root of Chicago, and Eliel Saarinen of Detroit.[36] The exhibition was scheduled to run for six weeks, but on the first Sunday after it opened 10,000 people came to see it, and it was held over for half a year. Thus, in 1929, when Art Deco architecture had already begun to make a strong showing in New York City and had already been accepted by the public, the Metropolitan Museum put its stamp of approval on it.

The Viennese Influence

Since the 1925 exposition took place in Paris, there has often been an automatic assumption that Art Deco represents a populariza-

Josef Hoffmann, Palais Stoclet, Brussels, 1905-11.

tion of Cubism. One can point to the Cubists' transformation of a coherent picture space into an oscillating surface, a feature apparent in some examples of Art Deco ornament. On the other hand, flat, two-dimensional articulation of ornament is also common in Art Deco. And specific details of the Art Deco style—its jagged points, chevrons, triangles, and tightly packed fields of flowers—have no precedent in Cubism at all.

Several characteristics of Art Deco have their origin in Art Nouveau—not the sinuous type of Art Nouveau, but the Glasgow type and especially the Viennese version, the Secession style. The Secession style was perhaps more architectonic in a traditional sense than any other form of the Art Nouveau. Its architecture retained a clear, classically-inspired form; richness was achieved by using precious materials like marble, lush colors, and architectural ornament that usually appeared in restricted areas or was subjected to a regular geometric structure without the whiplash that marked the Art Nouveau style in most of its other phases. The major architects of the Secession style were Otto Wagner, Joseph Olbrich, and Josef Hoffmann.[37] More important than specific works of these architects in the promulgation of the Secession style was the Wiener Werkstätte (Vienna Workshop) founded in 1903 under Hoffmann's leadership. It produced arts and crafts objects designed by artists and architects and executed in its own workshops—by 1905 the Werkstätte employed more than one hundred workers.[38] Right from the beginning, its products—whether jewelry, fabrics, or china—could easily be con-

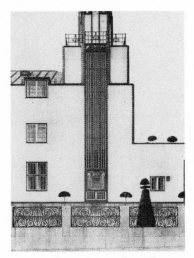

Palais Stoclet, exterior detail.

fused with Art Deco objects. There are the same bold fabric designs, pendants set in geometric frames, and rectangular and polygonal porcelain objects with vertical sides. Exemplifying the unified Wiener Werkstätte style is the Palais Stoclet in Brussels (1905-11), a villa designed by Hoffmann and with interior decoration by Wiener Werkstätte artists like Gustav Klimt. The building's exterior is fairly restrained; the smooth, marble-veneered walls with corners and windows emphasized by a dark metallic molding anticipate the "cool" materials favored in the thirties. The stepped tower with its Neoclassical statues and urns heaped with metallic flowers prefigures other aspects of the Art Deco style. The dining room of the Palais Stoclet was of yellow marble with a black and white marble floor and held a severe-looking set of dining chairs with octagonal metal sconces on the wall. The austerity was broken only by a magnificent frieze, designed by Klimt, that consisted of a mosaic of majolica, hammered metal, enameled pieces, opals, coral, and other stones.[39] Sheldon Cheney, in *The New World Architecture* of 1930, calls Viennese design "the smartest examples of Modernism thus far achieved. The Viennese seem to have made elegance the first test of success." Of Hoffmann's Palais Stoclet he writes that with its smooth, metal-trimmed walls it must have made carriages look out of date, and that motor cars would look completely appropriate next to it.[40]

Josef Hoffmann, Palais Stoclet dining room.

In 1915 the Wiener Werkstätte was joined by Dagobert Peche,
a young architect who brought to the geometric style of the Secession a playful manner in a Rococo spirit and prefigured in
many of his designs the more frivolous side of Art Deco.[41] Wiener
Werkstätte products were well known in Europe through their
frequent illustration in periodicals and through such exhibitions
as the 1914 Werkbund exhibition in Cologne at which Hoffmann
and Peche had each designed a room for the Austrian pavilion.
The Wiener Werkstätte also opened up branches in several cities,
including Berlin, Zurich (this shop was designed and run by
Peche from 1917 until 1919), and New York. The New York
branch, on Fifth Avenue, was opened in 1919 under the man-

agement of the Austrian-born Joseph Urban.[42] The shop itself was a showpiece of the Secession style, and although it was not a financial success, its influence on New York architecture and design was important.[43] Leon Solon, a friend of Kahn's, wrote in 1923, in an article on the New York Wiener Werkstätte in the *Architectural Record*, that its style is usually called Art Nouveau but that it anticipates a new decorative feeling in architecture.[44] And Paul Frankl, like Urban an Austrian and active as a designer in New York, says: ". . . Joseph Urban's initiative in bringing the work of the Wiener Werkstätte to America may be considered one of the initial stepping stones in the development of our modern art movement. It succeeded in bringing many ideas, if only for a time, before the American public."[45]

The German and Central European Influence

Despite Germany's absence from the 1925 Paris exposition, its influence was not totally diminished. Not all roads led to Paris, and architects had their own ways of keeping informed. Ely Jacques Kahn, for example, during trips to Europe visited exhibitions not only in Paris, but also in Austria and Germany.[46] There seems to have been a general interest in German architecture, for an editor of *The American Architect* reports in 1925 that readers had requested illustrations of more German work.[47]

César Klein, bedroom for Wolfgang Gurlitt, Berlin, 1919.

Walter Gropius, Sommerfeld
House, Berlin, 1921-22,
stairwell.

What was of interest to American architects in German architecture of this period was probably not the works in the International Style, nor the more utopian designs of Expressionist architects.[48] It was more likely the popularized versions of Expressionism that seem to prefigure the Art Deco style of the later twenties. For example, in 1919 the Expressionist artist César Klein designed a bedroom for a Berlin house that seems like full-fledged Art Deco but in its German context is classified as Expressionist. And Walter Gropius' Sommerfeld House in Berlin of 1921-22, in its exterior and especially interior decorations carved by Bauhaus students, has as its *leitmotiv* triangles and chevrons, including triangular lighting fixtures—the very forms that became typical in the Art Deco style.

The faceted, crystalline ceilings of Voorhees, Gmelin & Walker's Irving Trust and Salvation Army buildings (54, 36) were prefigured in Bruno Taut's recreation room for a single men's residence in Berlin of 1919-20, in a dance casino at the Scala Palace in Berlin by Walter Würzbach and the sculptor Rudolf Belling of circa 1920, and in a restaurant used in Fritz Lang's 1922 film *Dr. Mabuse, the Gambler.*

Fiske Kimball in *American Architecture* (1928) wrote of the German influence: ". . . a reflux from abroad is favoring the

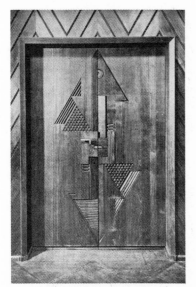

Sommerfeld House, detail of carved door by Joost Schmidt, a Bauhaus student.

drift from the classic. Certain American artists have recognized the creative liberty secured by the Germans, and are trying to free themselves from the bondage of academic detail while preserving the American heritage of simplicity and unity of form."[49]

Perhaps most congenial to the Beaux-Arts trained New York architects was a conservative interpretation of the Expressionist style which appeared in the so-called North German brick style, which resurrected the Hanseatic Gothic tradition of brick architecture and added some Expressionist overtones. Ornament is usually ingrained; that is, the structural unit, the brick itself, is used to introduce decoration by varying color tonalities and by changing the normal alignment of the bricks so that they project in angular patterns from the wall. The overall impression this type of architecture produces is of an earthy, hand-crafted texture. The March 1925 issue of *The American Architect* published illustrations of North German Expressionism—Fritz Höger's Chilehaus (1922-23) and Hans and Oskar Gerson's Ballinhaus (1923), both in Hamburg.[50] The Expressionism of these brick structures was often mixed with such Gothicizing features as triangular piers, as in Höger's Chilehaus; this device came to be used in many Art Deco buildings in New York as well.[51]

Peter Behrens, to whom Gropius, Mies, and Corbusier had been apprenticed during his earlier, better-known classicizing period,

Restaurant scene with faceted ceiling from Fritz Lang's *Dr. Mabuse, the Gambler*, 1922.

Fritz Höger, Chilehaus,
Hamburg, 1922-23, detail
showing some of the brick
textures.

Höger, Chilehaus, general
view.

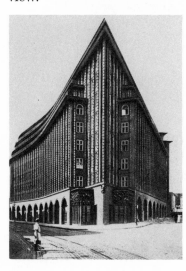

after World War I also turned to a medievalizing Expressionism. His "Dombauhütte" (cathedral lodge) designed for the Munich crafts show of 1922 is symptomatic. Although the medieval masons' lodge was only the workshop associated with the construction of a cathedral, Behrens designed his in the form of a chapel with interwoven, angular forms of varicolored brick suggesting a return to the integration of crafts with architecture and a superiority of handicrafts over machine work.[52] In Behrens' design for the I. G. Farben Dyeworks at Höchst, executed between 1920 and 1924, the Medieval and Expressionist styles appear split: the exterior of this large industrial complex is conservatively articulated in a Neomedieval style, whereas the multilevel entrance hall is an Expressionist transformation of a soaring Gothic interior. The material is brick throughout. On the exterior, brick is used in horizontal bands. In the hall the brick colors intensify toward the top, from a blue-green below to an orange-yellow above, a crescendo effect that terminates in star-shaped skylights. This building was illustrated in *The American Architect* in 1925, almost as soon as it had been completed,[53] and it may well be the source for the shaded brick structures in New York.

Germany was not the only source for vaguely Expressionist, medievalizing, folkloristic, or handicraft tendencies in early Art Deco architecture. A national romanticism seems to have af-

Peter Behrens, I. G. Farben,
Höchst, 1920-24, main hall.

fected the old Hanseatic League from Scandinavia to Holland during the first quarter of the century. Ragnar Östberg's Stockholm Town Hall with its vernacular overtones (1909-23), P. V. Jensen Klint's Expressionist Grundvig Church in Copenhagen (1913, 1921-26), and Eliel Saarinen's classicizing Helsinki railroad station (1905-14) are all part of this romantic and colorful style,[54] as are J. M. van der Meij's proto-Art Deco Scheepvaarthuis in Amsterdam (1912-16) and the more idiosyncratic expressionist works of such Amsterdam School architects as Michel de Klerk and Willem Dudok.[55] De Klerk's hous-

Van der Meij,
Scheepvaarthuis.

ing was illustrated here in 1922 in the *Journal of the American Institute of Architects* and in 1925 in the *Architectural Record*.[56] And in 1923 the *Architectural Forum* had shown some buildings by Dudok.[57] Cheney in *The New World Architecture* had this to say about Dutch architecture: ". . . for nearly a decade—until Germany actively resumed building and overtook her two or three years ago—Holland showed the most Modernistic face to the world of any of the nations. And for a new architecture with a most pronounced national or racial flavor you must even today go to the Dutch cities."[58] After 1927, when the Art Deco style in New York intensified, the volume of European material shown in American periodicals also increased. Evidence of the influence of the Expressionist brick style is especially strong in Voorhees, Gmelin & Walker's Western Union Building (27; 1928-30), with its unusual animated-looking brick panels.

A further aspect, the use of vivid color, found especially in the earlier examples of Art Deco, can be related to German Expressionist architecture in general, not just to the North German brick style.[59] Influenced by such Expressionist artists as Kandinsky, Bruno Taut had used vibrant colors in his housing projects from 1914 on.[60] Behrens' already mentioned use of glazed bricks in the interior of the Hoechst Dyeworks is another instance of an Expressionist color scheme. Many publications in America testify to a similar interest. Leon Solon published in the *Architectural Record* of 1922 a series of articles on polychromy in architecture.[61] And although they dealt largely with the use of color in Greek architecture (in this sense they still reflected the Beaux-Arts taste of the early twenties), they also introduced the general idea of a brightly ornamented architecture. Solon's essays were subsequently published as a book in 1924.[62] In an article in a 1921 issue of the *Architectural Record*, Alfred Bossom, in discussing the work of the artist Nicholas Roerich, claimed that more color had been appearing in recent architecture.[63] And one wonders whether it was Roerich's idea to have the exterior of the Master Institute and Riverside Museum (formerly Roerich Museum) shade from a purple brick at the base to a light grey brick at the top. Another article, "Architectural Polychromy" by C. Howard Walker, appeared in the March 1923 issue of the *Architectural Record*,[64] and in October 1925 W. Francklyn Paris, in reviewing the 1925 Paris exposition, wrote that "expressionists" held center stage and goes on to characterize the new style. He believed that mass in modern architecture must remain undisguised, that it must consist of straight lines and sharp angles; and since applied

Hans Poelzig, Grosses
Schauspielhaus, Berlin,
1919, foyer.

decoration had become taboo (his analysis in this respect does not seem to describe the style of the 1925 Paris show), he called for color and rich materials to take its place.[65] In a similar vein Ely Jacques Kahn wrote in "On the Use of Color" of 1928 that color contrasts in architecture could eliminate carving and crockets. In another essay the following year, "On Decoration and Ornament," Kahn wrote that color must be used in proportion to the distance of the observer.[66] This indicates that perceptual effects of color were considered, that is, the intensity of the color used depended on the distance it was to be from street level and the observer. A concern for color is also apparent in most of Raymond Hoods' work up until about 1930. The Daily News Building has piers of white vitreous brick with spandrels of dark red and dull red brick patterns, and the window shades were red to harmonize with the spandrels. And Hood's blue-green glazed terra-cotta spandrels in the McGraw-Hill Building were described in 1931 as producing a good "atmospheric" quality under all types of weather conditions.[67] And as late as 1934 Sheldon Cheney, in his *Expressionism in Art*, wrote that although Victorian luxuriousness was missed in modern architecture, the bareness of the new architecture could be enriched in the idiom appropriate to the time by using a greater range of color.[68]

In German Expressionist architecture the interest in using color sprang originally from the desire to use colored glass that would transform light into a mystical experience, a light mysticism comparable to Gothic mysticism. However, in utopian Expressionist projects this signaled not so much religious feeling as a spiritual transformation of society. In Expressionism concern for light and for color usually went together. When building was again possible after World War I and the inflation that had followed, glass was usually found to be too costly, so that the dream of a colored glass architecture was changed into polychrome brick or colored stucco surfaces. Indirect lighting, with the source of light not revealed, often became a substitute in executed buildings for light seen through colored glass. A master of early examples of indirect lighting was Hans Poelzig. His Grosses Schauspielhaus of 1919 in Berlin uses indirect lighting for the columns of the foyer and in the theater itself. This was shown in a 1923 issue of *The American Architect*.[69] The use of indirect lighting of lobbies and the dramatic nighttime lighting of pinnacles, such as in the Barclay-Vesey Building, the RCA Victor Building, and the Chanin Building, is an effect that may have been borrowed from the Expressionist projects for glass architecture illuminated at night.[70] Or it may be a device borrowed from the theater. As early as 1921 Kenneth Macgowan, in *The Theatre of Tomorrow* (a book found in Voorhees, Gmelin & Walker's library), discusses Poelzig's Grosses Schauspielhaus and his set designs for *The Golem*, and makes a special point of German stage lighting as practiced by Max Reinhardt, Adolphe Appia, and Gordon Craig. The use of chiaroscuro lighting producing deep spatial effects is contrasted with Leon Bakst's flat, almost two-dimensional stage sets. The latter are depicted as somewhat outmoded.[71] In the January 1925 issue of the *Architectural Record*, in an article on "New Dimensions in Architectural Effects," Herbert Kroly wrote that the new zoning law was not nearly as important as the new effect that could be achieved through using color and light. Referring to the gilding used on Raymond Hood's American Radiator Building of 1924, he writes: "The gilding of these stories suggests . . . bewildering possibilities as to the future use of surfaces with colors, glows, and lights in order to convert the high places of New York, as seen from distant streets, into a wonderland of elaborate, fanciful and vivid masses and patterns."[72] Again, as for Kahn, the stated reason was to make the tops of skyscrapers visible at ground level and from far away. Harvey Wiley Corbett, in a 1930 article, "Design in Office Buildings" in *The Architectural Forum*, further reinforces a call for nocturnal lighting: he demands a wider use of color and proposes that buildings be flooded with harmonizing hues at night.[73] Such dramatic effects, when applied to an office building, are no longer comparable in intention to German Expressionism. They appear here simply as devices borrowed from the theater, dramatic devices that seem to coalesce with the equally theatrical sculptural and ornamental program of several Art Deco buildings; the drama of life in the modern metropolis is depicted as taking place not in its churches, schools, or city hall but in the office skyscraper. Kahn, in his essay "On the Use of Color," writes that the ". . . Dream of a colored city, buildings in harmonious tones making great masses of beautiful patterns, may be less of a vision if the enterprising city developer suspects the result."[74] This is Kahn, the public relations man, speaking about a dream world with commercial value.

Some American artists, architects, and historians were familiar enough with central European architecture and design to allow them to see the Paris 1925 show not as the first creative outburst of a new style, but as the eclectic amalgam of styles that it was. This is clear from an essay by Leon Solon; he writes that the exhibition has fallen short of expectations because unusual forms were procured at any cost. He acknowledges the desire to create advertising value, but sees in much of what was shown a French interpretation of central and northern European styles.[75] Leo Friedlander, an architectural sculptor like Solon, wrote in a 1927 *Architectural Forum* that the seed of the new movement "was sown in Austria 28 years ago. Its influence first spread to Germany, then to Scandinavia, Holland, Finland, Servia, Belgium and France."[76] And Ely Jacques Kahn in a 1929 issue of *Creative Art* wrote:

It is commonplace to the ignorant to assume that so-called modernism is a mushroom growth of the day, possibly a recollection of 1925 in Paris—still more dimly a shaking of the old bones of the L'Art Nouveau. So much has already been said in this connection that it is trite to refer to the thirty years of development in Austria, Germany, Belgium, and the more recent Renaissance in France.[77]

The historian Fiske Kimball in his *American Architecture* of 1928 stated the same idea more briefly. He believed that an "impulse from abroad was given by the Paris exposition of decorative arts in 1925, where surviving elements of the *art nouveau*, which had remained in solution, were precipitated by reagents from Vienna."[78] And Sheldon Cheney in *The New World Architecture* of 1930, discussing the new European style, is the harshest critic of the 1925 exhibition:

And why is there no weighty evidence from France? As early as 1925, Paris spread out the buildings of the Exposition of Decorative Arts, avowedly to bring to focus contemporary French effort outside the traditional styles—and to bring world Modernism into agreement with the graceful French talent. But that affair, and sporadic outcroppings here and there, . . . have only gone to show that outside a few inspired engineers and one or two imported radical architects, the impotent Beaux-Arts men still control France. Even the Exposition proved the French to be adapters of the Viennese thing, softening down the squared masses into sweeter and more graceful forms—with the sensuous delicacy of the Viennese touch a little spread toward the luxurious and grandiose. . . .
. . . The French Modernists, as a matter of fact, have fattened themselves a bit over-assiduously on the Blue-Danube seductive grace, until Paris passes on to the Americas and to England and points more remote a hall-marked French decorative mode that is really sweetened and popularized Viennese.[79]

Extending this food analogy, one might say that to Cheney the 1925 exhibition is Viennese pastry served up as gingerbread.

American Influence

As has been noted before, the Art Deco architect did not look only to Europe for inspiration. Within the American tradition the work of Louis Sullivan and Frank Lloyd Wright is central. Sullivan's use of a luxurious but tightly organized ornament within a generally classicizing massing of form can be seen as a prototype for comparable Art Deco features. His emphatic use of vertical piers with recessed spandrels is another element common in Art Deco skyscrapers. Further, Sullivan's accent on building entrance and building top by means of a dynamic ornament (usually spandrels are ornamented also, but with a pattern more rigid and geometric than that used for entrance and top) becomes general practice in most Art Deco skyscrapers.

The references among writers of the twenties to the wall as a veneer or a curtain[80] can be traced to ideas circulated by the Chicago School, ideas which, together with Sullivan's placement of architectural ornament, derive from the theories of the nineteenth-century German architect Gottfried Semper. John Wellborn Root translated and published one of Semper's essays—"Development of Architectural Style"—in the *Inland Architect* of 1890. Earlier, during a discussion of the Illinois State Association of Architects, published in the *Inland Architect* in 1887, Semper had been quoted by one of the speakers.[81] Louis Sullivan had been present at this meeting. Also, Dankmar Adler, Sullivan's partner, was fond of reciting Semperian *bons mots*. Semper in one of his essays on the evolution of architectural form, "The Four Elements of Architecture," had proposed four basic components: the hearth as the first social gathering place, the basement to raise the hearth off the damp ground, a roof with supporting poles to protect the fire against rain, and lastly an enclosure of textiles, animal skins, wattle or any other filler either hung from the frame or placed between the supporting poles.[82] These concepts, proposed to explain past architectural development, were often interpreted as a recipe for new architecture, hence the interest in creating curtain walls that look like woven tapestries (6A, 21A, 26G). Semper had also developed notions of dynamic distribution of ornament in architecture: areas of greatest dynamic stress (actual and apparent), such as entries and roof lines, were seen as being in tension and therefore received emphatic fields of decoration. Sullivan seems to have followed Semper in his organization of ornament.[83]

The use of extensive ornament at the ground floor and near the top in Art Deco buildings is thus tied to a nineteenth-century tradition that lends them scale at close range as well as from a distance and makes them appear less dehumanizing than the unarticulated top and the bland elevator lobby which characterize most current office buildings.

Frank Lloyd Wright, Midway Gardens, Chicago, 1914. Detail of inter-penetrating sculptural ornament and textured concrete blocks.

Frank Lloyd Wright, A. D. German Warehouse, Richland Center, Wisconsin, 1915. Detail of patterned blocks facing top storey.

Although Frank Lloyd Wright had not yet executed any of his skyscraper projects by the twenties, his influence on the Art Deco style was considerable and may be perceived in his very early development of an abstract, usually geometric ornament. This appeared first in the stained glass panels of his prairie houses, then in the tiles used in the Coonley House (1908) that imitate textile patterns, and it becomes part of an ingrained architectural ornament in the patterned concrete blocks of the Midway Gardens (1914), in the lava blocks of the Imperial Hotel (1916-22), and in the various concrete blocks for his California houses of the early twenties.[84] Both of Paul Frankl's books, *New Dimensions* of 1928 and *Form and Re-Form* of 1930, begin with illustrations from Wright's California houses.

Another American stylistic ingredient of Art Deco architecture, the Pre-Columbian influence, had been interpreted by Wright in his A. D. German Warehouse (1915) and in his Hollyhock House (1920). Wright's use of ornament within clearly defined zones and canted walls seems to have been inspired by Mayan architecture. However, there is little direct reference to any Pre-Columbian design in New York Art Deco,[85] except perhaps in the ornament of Edward Sibbert's Kress Building (106) and, possibly, the decorative detailing of Starrett & Van Vleck's Bloomingdale store (56). In Art Deco crafts the frequent stepped design of appliances and furniture is assumed to derive from Mayan or Aztec pyramids. Similar stepped formations in architecture, on the other hand, depend more likely on the New York City zoning law that required such setbacks.[86]

There was, though, in the Art Deco period a certain interest in primitivism, a tendency common among early twentieth-century styles. The 1923 *Architectural Record* carried an article titled "A

Frank Lloyd Wright, Hollyhock House, Hollywood, 1920.

Primitive Basis for Modern Architecture," which claimed that the American Indians were the first Cubists. However this claim was illustrated with works in a New Mexico Mission style.[87] An exceptional exoticism is the Egyptian cornice of Schwartz & Gross' apartment house on Central Park West (20B). More often references to primitive or exotic styles are difficult to classify and, at least in New York, they flourished more readily in interior decoration. Winold Reiss, an Austrian-born designer, executed two New York interiors, both no longer in existence, the Crillon Restaurant in peasant motifs[88] and the Congo Room at the Hotel Alamac with chairs whose backs consisted of flat panels in the shape of black and white aborigines and with walls covered with jungle murals and masks.[89]

Popular Cultural Influences

Because from its very beginning Art Deco was not an abstruse style, it not only drew inspiration from earlier architecture, but was especially open to influences from stage and screen in which high art had already been digested and popularized. *The American Architect* published in 1920 the following editorial:

The important motion picture producers are fast realizing the commercial value of good architecture. This fact is becoming evident in the recent presentation of "feature films." Among those legends which announce the various people who shared responsibility in the production of a scenario, it is becoming customary to include the name of the architect who designed the exteriors and planned the arrangement and decoration of rooms which serve as a background for the story. Architects will appreciate this recognition of their cooperation in these matters.[90]

This is an indication that architectural design was being made part of the film, and that architecture could affect public taste through film. In fact, in 1921 the *Journal of the American Institute of Architects* published an essay about *Caligari* and its use of exaggerated space and lighting.[91] Sets from the theater and film began, in fact, to influence taste, and designs by Norman Bel Geddes or Lee Simonson were as much discussed as the plays themselves.[92] And in 1922 the *Architectual Record* illustrated Claude Bragdon's and Norman Bel Geddes' theater design.[93]

The German Expressionist film was especially precocious in using artists and architects as set designers, and such films as *The Cabinet of Dr. Caligari* (1919) and *The Golem* (1920) contain many formal elements that came to be called Art Deco at a later time. *Caligari* was shown in the States in 1921, and although it was

Scene from *The Cabinet of Dr. Caligari* (Robert Wiene, director), 1919. This view shows the use of distorted space and exaggerated light and shadows.

Interior scene from *Caligari*. In contrast to the angular exterior setting, this shows softly rounded forms. Both formal treatments are ingredients of Art Deco.

seen by comparatively few people, it was nevertheless the most widely discussed film of the time. . . . "It is a matter of record that no picture, not even *The Birth of a Nation*, ever created quite as much comment, argument, and speculation in one month's time as did *The Cabinet of Dr. Caligari*."[94]

The Golem, with Expressionist sets designed by the architect Hans Poelzig, was also released here in 1921. Writing in *Theatre Magazine*, a reviewer said that "this is another of the spectacular German films that have recently been imported into this country, thereby breaking the nightly rest of Hollywood."[95] The impact of such films on Hollywod fostered an influx of European film-makers. Erté, the French designer, also came to Hollywood to do the sets for the film *Paris 25*.[96] A later film like Fritz Lang's *Metropolis* (1926) contained Art Deco details, especially in its interior architectural design (Lang had originally studied architecture before becoming a film director), but the views of his Metropolis with its ominous buildings, viaducts and overpasses, and airplanes whirring between skyscrapers prefigure the futuristic images of the modern metropolis later created by Hugh Ferris. In *Metropolis* the imagery of the modern city also has come full circle, for Lang was influenced in the creation of his sets by a view of the Manhattan skyline seen on a boat trip to the States in 1924:

Night view of city from *Metropolis* (Fritz Lang, director), 1926.

I first came to America briefly in 1924 and it made a great impression on me. The first evening, when we arrived, we were still enemy aliens so we couldn't leave the ship. It was docked somewhere on the West Side of New York. I looked into the streets—the glaring lights and the tall buildings—and there I conceived *Metropolis*.[97]

Night club entrance from *Metropolis*.

A large exhibit of contemporary design held at Macy's in 1928 and called "Art in Trade Exposition" (organized by the Art in Trade Club) brought many of the divergent sources of the Art Deco style together under one roof. There were rooms by the Austrian Josef Hoffmann, by the German Bruno Paul, by the Italian Gio Ponti, by French designers and design groups—Leleu, Dufrêne, and D.I.M.—by the New York architect Eugene Schoen, and by Kem Weber, a German who had settled in Los Angeles where he worked both as an architect and a Hollywood set designer.[98] The popularization of the Art Deco style through the Paris exposition of 1925, through films, and through the shows at Lord and Taylor's and Macy's in 1928 makes clear that from the beginning Art Deco was seen as a marketable modern style.

A Period of Science, Industry, and Business

What figure the poet might employ to describe the skyscraper, dwarfing the church, outpointing the cathedral spire, I do not know. There is an epic implication in man's defiance of the laws of gravity, and beauty in the naked lift of uprising steel and concrete. But the purpose of the skyscraper is not poetic. Perhaps Commercialism is a new God, only too powerful and too appealing, to Whom men are building today their largest, costliest, and most laudatory structures. In this service they are building higher and ever higher, concentrating more and more activity into less of ground space, stealing light and air from their neighbors, piously recording in their structures the Exploitation that is [a] right-hand attribute of Commercialism.

At any rate, the skyscraper is the typical building of the twentieth century. New York City . . . sees the rise of scores of business buildings larger, more honest in methods of construction and in purpose (for the cathedral in coming times, as now, can be little more than a show place, a piece of insincerity), and more expressive of contemporary living. Business rules the world today, and as long as business can best be served where many offices are concentrated in one small area, in buildings designed as machines for the efficient discharge of buying, selling, trading, banking, law disputes, gambling, and exploitation, business architecture will be supreme.[99]

Contemporary writers agreed in characterizing their period. For Edwin Avery Park, writing in *New Backgrounds for a New Age* of 1927, America was a new world of science, industry, and business;[100] he believed that American art of the future would be a reflection of industrial democracy. Paul T. Frankl wrote similarly in *New Dimensions* of 1928: "Our age is one of invention, machinery, industry, science, and commerce."[101] For both writers the times were distinguished by a triumvirate of science, industry, and business, not art. In 1928 Frankl was still overwhelmed by the rapid pace of industrialized society, and he saw art as an antidote to the world at large: "The great complexity of things about us is quite worrying. Human nature cannot keep pace with modern invention. And, while complexity is a characteristic of our mechanical lives, it is the opposite of this that we seek for in aesthetic enjoyment. The opposite of complexity is simplicity."[102] But by 1930, in *Form and Re-Form*, he seems to have come to terms with complexity and speed. Instead of counteracting it in aesthetic expression, he now proposes to articulate it. For him the spirit of American democracy manifests itself in freedom, frankness, freshness, directness, compression, and speed.[103] The subversion of traditional values by the frenetic rhythms of science and industry had not even been questioned by Park, who had written: "Houses are less important than motor cars, and furniture less again than hot water, thermostats and scientific kitchens. Utility and mobility we seek."[104]

New industrial materials were beginning to make an impact on architecture, particularly interiors and furniture design, in a manner reminiscent of the Victorian period's unabashed and inventive use of materials like cast iron and papier-mâché for furniture. Paul Frankl wrote admiringly of this trend that "industrial chemistry today rivals alchemy! Base materials are transmuted into marvels of new beauty."[105] Formica was used for interior walls: vitrolite, a heavy black glass, was employed especially in hotels, restaurants, and theaters (as in Frederick Kiesler's Film Guild Cinema, for instance). Monel metal, a copper and nickel alloy, was used for soda fountains and furniture trim. Bakelite was probably among the best-known of the early plastics and was used for a wide variety of manufactured goods. Synthetic cork plates could be employed as wall or floor coverings, and aluminum leaf replaced silver leaf and was used for the ceilings of the staircases in the Chrysler Building.[106]

By around 1930 the designs of Art Deco architects began to be affected by an overwhelming realization that the machine and industry are overriding factors in modern life.[107] Sheldon Cheney's estimate in *The New World Architecture* is brightly optimistic:

There will ultimately be machine-developed energy to solve all men's work problems, with no more labor than is involved in passing control. The elements themselves will be tamed, weather tempered, transportation become effortless, cleanliness universal, the works of the intellect and of the artistic faculties will be transported instantaneously to all. Living will be speeded, concentrated, regulated, as never before.

There is no turning back. There is no hindering the swiftness of humanity's advance toward that time. No one can foresee the organization that will turn all this to the good of the human soul, when the old pivots on which individual life has turned—labor, making a living, money, protective nationalistic governments—are scrapped. We only know that increasingly now the problem of nobly utilizing leisure time becomes all-important. We are past the possibility of challenging the machine, of curbing it, of attempting escape from it. We must live in a way that crowds into a week what used to be the experiences of a year, that makes a half-hour's work of what used to occupy our grandparents for a day. We must move by machinery, communicate by it—live by it.[108]

Architects now turned to a machine aesthetic, as the Futurists, Constructivists, and International Style architects had done before them. As in the latter groups, the machine was mythologized and romanticized. No direct influence from these movements is suggested. Antonio Sant'Elia's Futurist architectural designs of 1913-14 were not publicized in America. If we can speak of Futurist or Constructivist tendencies in the later Art Deco style, they came indirectly through International Style architecture, which by the thirties was beginning to affect the Art Deco style. The hand-crafted, Expressionist-influenced, and exotic quality of the earlier Art Deco style disappeared and was replaced by severer, Neoclassic forms with much less ornament and almost no color. Upward-rushing, Gothic-inspired piers are no longer the norm. Horizontal features appear more frequently—in part adapted from the International Style and in part suggesting the streaking image of vehicles flashing by. Terra-cotta decoration gives way to smoothly articulated surfaces with an occasional rounded, streamlined corner, sheathed in shining metal. Such streamlining effects are often seen as having been influenced by similar methods in car design. By 1931 streamlining had affected architecture, as in the entrance to the McGraw-Hill Building (82A) and in the foyer of Joseph Urban's auditorium for the New School (51E). But strangely, as late as 1932 Norman Bel Geddes was still complaining that streamlining had not yet made any inroads into commercial car design.[109] Streamlined forms had actually been used by Eric Mendelsohn in sketches and executed buildings in the teens and throughout the twenties, most of which had been published here by 1930. Mendelsohn had wanted to suggest in a generalized sense the dynamics of modern industry; the one executed example

Eric Mendelsohn, sketches for industrial buildings, most of which contain streamlined forms, from Sheldon Cheney, *The New World Architecture*, 1930.

that prefigures a specific motif of the later streamlined style is his interior of the Universum Cinema (1927-28) in Berlin. Its parallel horizontal triple-line bands leading toward the screen appear to be a direct precedent for the similar motif in the entrance to the McGraw-Hill Building.

When Mendelsohn visited the United States in 1924 he spent two days as the guest of Frank Lloyd Wright at Taliesin. While on a walk near Taliesin they drew designs in the sand on the banks of a river, Wright a garage with an imaginary superstructure, Mendelsohn a sketch with rounded contours. That evening and the next morning Mendelsohn made architectural sketches from which Wright selected several for himself.[110] The younger architect's impact on Wright can perhaps be seen in some of the latter's streamlined designs for the Broadacre City project and the Johnson Wax Administration Building, both of the thirties.

Also, in 1934 the Museum of Modern Art held a "Machine Art" exhibition. In the catalogue for the show, Alfred H. Barr elevated the product of the machine to a Platonic archetype:

The beauty of machine art is in part the abstract beauty of straight lines and circles made into actual tangible surfaces and solids by means of tools, lathes and rules and squares. In Plato's day the tools were simple handworker's implements but today, as a result of the perfection of modern materials and the precision of modern instruments, the modern machine-made object approaches far more closely and more frequently those pure shapes the contemplation of which Plato calls the first of the "pure pleasures."[111]

The austerity and machine imagery of the later Art Deco style with its greyer, more impersonal look (see Cross & Cross' Tiffany Building or Corbett's Criminal Courts Building, both of 1939), also fits in better with the Depression. The lushness of the earlier style might have looked too frivolous during the thirties, and the dramatic pyrotechnics of the earlier Art Deco gave way to a stylization of the workaday world.

The End of a Period

What was responsible for the demise of Art Deco architecture? The Depression played a large role. By the late thirties most of the Art Deco structures going up were no longer corporate but mostly federal or municipal buildings. Then the beginning of World War II resulted in a steep decline of new building.

However, even before the onset of World War II, taste was beginning to shift in favor of the International Style. Starting in 1932, with the publication of Henry-Russell Hitchcock's and Philip Johnson's *The International Style* and the already-mentioned Museum of Modern Art International Architecture exhibition, it became clear that a European style had evolved that was regarded as more advanced by the most prestigious architectural historians. In the exhibition catalogue for the Museum of Modern Art show, the Art Deco architects were, as mentioned earlier, singled out as the adversaries of the new style. In another Museum of Modern Art publication, *What Is Modern Architecture?* of 1942, the characteristics assigned to the International Style by Hitchcock and Johnson are still stated unequivocally as design principles for modern architecture in general. However, by 1944, in the catalogue of yet another Museum of Modern Art exhibit, *Built in USA—1932-1944*, the assurance of the earlier statements is beginning to be qualified and some doubt about the universal validity of the International Style appears. Elizabeth Mock, looking back to the Museum of Modern Art catalogue of 1932 in her foreword, finds that the analysis of aesthetic principles is still correct; however, she goes on to say:

But the book had its weakness. Although modern materials and construction and modern living preferences were recognized as the basis of the new esthetics, there is little hint of their endless possibilities for development, nor of the effect such development would inevitably have upon design. The Museum placed great importance on "volume," achieved through non-committal, dematerialized wall planes, absence of projecting cornice, flush doors and flush ribbon windows, whereas modern architecture has always had, at least potentially, a freedom and flexibility far beyond those limits.[112]

In any case, the Museum of Modern Art had played an important role in paving the way for the acceptance of the International Style in this country. In 1933, shortly after the International Style had been pinpointed and codified by Hitchcock and Johnson, Talbot Hamlin published a succinct attack on it in an essay in *The American Architect* called "The International Style Lacks the Essence of Great Architecture." He begins bitterly:

The climax of the propaganda that has surrounded the birth of an architecture of today has been the development of a movement called the International Style. This, its sponsors claim, is architecture indeed, the only valid method of building under the present social system. To this International Style as to the god of a new religion they offer a service of adulation artfully compounded of the methods of modern publicity, and the ethical and religious passion of a Ruskin.[113]

And comparing the salient features of great architecture of the past with those of the International Style, Hamlin writes:

. . . the sense stimulus is the primary element; and the more intellectual the content that is required for its appreciation, the more esoteric the art. The layman—for all great architecture is sooner or later loved by the layman—is not an engineer, a philosopher, or a sociologist, except in the most elementary manner. . . . He likes to have a feeling that things "work." But it's a qualitative, not a quantitative, interest. And it is true of both Greek and Gothic architectures that they appeal to this "qualitative" and not "quantitative" kind of thought. The layman can make them his own. And this is distinctly not true of the International Style, which aims most definitely at the other ideal.

It is not quantitative functionalism that is at the root of great architecture. It is not abstruse intellectual content of any kind. . . . It is not conformity to any theory. It is never the result of labored and self-conscious puritanism. It is never a denial of joy in life.

Examination of Greek and Gothic work, it seems, reveals an exuberance of color and form that is instinct with the delight of creation. It is not enough merely to build, these architectures seem to say, nor even to build well and with at least approximate honesty. Human desires demand more; over this framework, within it, imagination must play richly, not only to arrange, but to decorate, yet so beautifully that decoration itself shall seem to flow out of necessary form. To be beautiful, gracious, enticing—to take the bare limbs of building and make them flower like cherry trees in spring—is not this the engendering power of great architecture?

Thus great architecture has disciplines that are more stimuli than inhibitions. It can be helped, but never created, by structural expression; yet structural expression carried to the limit would often spoil it. . . . The root of great architecture is like the root of any created beauty, deep in the matrix of human consciousness. It is spontaneity, delight in form. It is a superfluity—almost always a sense of "more than enough." It is the play of creative minds that makes living and building a delight as well as a task. It is the dance of Siva.

Can it be that the International Style has never learned how to play?[114]

Using Hamlin's definition, we could say that if the International Style is one of "less is more," then Art Deco is a style of "more than enough."

A Skyscraper Fantasy

Let us end with a fantasy to end all Art Deco fantasies. When Frank Lloyd Wright was excluded from participation in the Chicago Century of Progress Fair to be held in 1933, he was invited by the American Union of Decorative Artists and Craftsmen to address them at Town Hall. Before the meeting Raymond Hood (one of the commissioners of the Chicago Fair) took him to dinner at the Crillon restaurant (designed by Winold Reiss). Afterwards, at Town Hall, Wright delineated three hypothetical proposals for fair architecture.[115] One of these, for a skyscraper, seems like the archetypal Art Deco multi-functional, theatrical, science-fiction building:

Build a great skyscraper in which the Empire State Building might stand free in a central interior court-space which would be devoted to all the resources of the modern elevator. . . .

Instead of glass for enclosure—some of our many light, transparent glass substitutes might be used. The multitudinous areas thus created could be let to the various exhibitors. The entire feature of the top stories could be garden observatories, pleasure places. . . . This tower construction of steel might rise from the triple-decked parking terraces, one corner of the terraces projecting and extending into the lake two ways at right angles to make piers and harbors for all water craft. Beneath the lake nearby where the reflections of the tower would fall, powerful jets of the lake itself rising by way of inserted power pumps to great height. All to be illuminated by modern light-projecting apparatus, projecting toward the tower and projecting from it. The lake thus at contingent points becoming a series of great fountains irradiated by light.

The Lake Front Park itself would thus become merely landscape adjunct to the great modern structure . . . about a half mile high.

The clouds might naturally or artificially drift across its summit. Or effects be created by aeroplanes laying down colored ribbons of smoke to drift across it.[116]

Rosemarie Haag Bletter

NOTES

1. Edwin Avery Park, *New Backgrounds for a New Age* (New York: Harcourt, Brace & Co., 1927), p. 50.
2. Paul T. Frankl, *Form and Re-Form* (New York: Harper & Brothers, 1930), p. 77.
3. Louis H. Sullivan, "The Tall Office Building Artistically Considered," reprinted in *Kindergarten Chats and Other Writings* (New York: Wittenborn, 1968), p. 205.
4. Sullivan had anticipated such later massing in his unexecuted design for a Fraternity Temple of 1891.
5. Sullivan, p. 206.
6. John Ruskin, *The Stones of Venice* (London: Smith, Elder & Co., 1851), vol. I, pp. 59-60. For further discussion of Ruskin's theory of ornament see Kristine Ottesen Garrigan, *Ruskin on Architecture—His Thought and Influence* (Madison: University of Wisconsin Press, 1973).
7. Ruskin, p. 238.
8. Talbot Faulkner Hamlin, "Is Originality Leading Us Into a New Victorianism?" *American Architect*, 141 (Feb. 1932), 70.
9. Ely Jacques Kahn, "The Province of Decoration in Modern Design," *Creative Art*, 5 (Dec. 1929), 886.
10. Forrest F. Lisle, Jr., "Chicago's 'Century of Progress' Exposition: The Moderne as Democratic, Popular Culture," abstract of paper presented at Twenty-Fifth Annual Meeting of the Society of Architectural Historians, San Francisco, January 26-30, 1972 (part of a program on Moderne Architecture, chaired by David S. Gebhard), *Society of Architectural Historians Journal*, 31:3 (Oct. 1972), 230.
11. Ibid.
12. To date there are two publications dealing with architecture. One is David Gebhard and Harriette von Breton, *Kem Weber—The Moderne in Southern California 1920 through 1941* (Santa Barbara: The Art Galleries, University of California, 1969). The same text was reprinted in David Gebhard, "The Moderne in the U.S. 1920-1941," *Architectural Association Quarterly*, 2 (July 1970), 4-20. The illustrations, however, are not the same as in the *Kem Weber* catalogue—the former illustrate the text on the Moderne in Southern California. Gebhard has also written a brief text for *The Richfield Building: 1928-68* (Los Angeles: Atlantic Richfield Company, 1970).
13. For example, Theodore Menten in his *The Art Deco Style* (New York: Dover, 1972) includes Corbusier's Voisin Plan, Gropius' Teachers' Housing at the Dessau Bauhaus, and Bruno Taut's exhibition hall at Magdeburg in Art Deco. And Yvonne Brunhammer in *The Nineteen Twenties Style* (London: Paul Hamlyn, 1966) calls her section on architecture simply "The In-

ternational Style" and proceeds to discuss the Werkbund, Gropius, and Taut as part of Art Deco.

14. Terminology is best discussed in Bevis Hillier, *Art Deco* (London: Studio Vista, 1968), p. 10 ff. The most comprehensive bibliography on Art Deco crafts appears in Bevis Hillier, *The World of Art Deco* exhibition catalogue, Minneapolis Institute of Arts, 1971.

15. Park still refers in 1927 to the new movement as "modernist" (p. 7). However, the following year Paul Frankl in *New Dimensions* (New York: Payson & Clarke, 1928) refers to "modernistic" effects (p. 18), and Leon Solon in "The Park Avenue Building, New York City," (*Architectural Record*, 63 (April 1928), 289-301) uses the terms "modernist" and "Modernistic." By 1932 the Museum of Modern Art in a catalogue for the *Modern Architecture International Exhibition* of 1932 refers several times to the "modernistic style," now in a perjorative sense.

16. See Gebhard text of *Kem Weber*.

17. Editorial, "A Regional Style of Architecture," *American Architect*, 117 (Feb. 4, 1920), 151-52.

18. While most authors agree that 1925 represents a central date, there is no clear indication why specific dates for the beginning of the style were chosen: Giulia Veronesi in *Style and Design, 1909-1929* (New York: Braziller, 1968) begins her discussion with the Art Nouveau style; Brunhammer, like Veronesi, sees the beginning of the style in 1909, but her stated reason is that 1909 is the date of Peter Behrens' AEG factory and the first Futurist manifesto (what these have to do with Art Deco is never explained); and Martin Battersby in *The Decorative Twenties* (New York: Walker & Co., 1969) fixes the beginning at 1910, although nearly all his illustrations are from the twenties.

19. *Modern Architecture—International Exhibition*, p. 13.

20. Veronesi, p. 219, and Rudolph Rosenthal and Helena Ratzka, *The Story of Modern Applied Art* (New York: Harper & Brothers, 1948), p. 77.

21. The Werkbund exerted its influence through its periodical, *Die Form*, through the Werkbund yearbook, and through exhibitions. See Julius Posener, *Anfänge des Funktionalismus—Von Arts and Crafts zum Deutschen Werkbund* (Berlin: Ullstein Bauwelt Fundamente, 1964). And Ulrich Conrads, editor, *Programmes and Manifestoes on 20th-century Architecture*, transl. by Michael Bullock (London: Lund Humphries, 1970).

22. Elie Richard, "Genèse d'une Exposition," Exposition Internationale des Arts Décoratifs et Industriels Modernes, Paris, Avril-Octobre 1925, *Catalogue Général Officiel* (Paris: Imprimerie de Vaugirard [1925]), unpaged. This also contains a map of the exhibition. See also Battersby, p. 17 and Judith Applegate, *Art Deco* (New York: Finch College Museum of Art, 1970), unpaged.

23. *Report of Commission appointed by the Secretary of Commerce to visit and report upon the Intl. Exposition of Modern Decorative and Industrial Art in Paris 1925*, p. 16.

24. Frankl, *Form and Re-Form*, p. 1.

25. *Report of Commission* . . . , p. 17.

26. Veronesi, p. 219.

27. *Le Corbusier und Pierre Jeanneret*, ed. and transl. by O. Stonorov and W. Boesiger (Zurich: Dr. H. Girsberger & Co., 1930), vol. I, pp. 100 and 102. It is really not very surprising that the commission erected this fence since it was part of Corbusier's program in the pavilion to reject the decorative arts.

28. It is also curious that, although the exposition was to be of decorative *and* industrial arts, there was in fact very little industrial art shown.

29. Further exceptions to the decorative frenzy of most of the pavilions were the designs by Tony Garnier and Auguste Perret.

30. Ely Jacques Kahn, unpublished manuscript, Avery Library, Columbia University, section II, p. 32.

31. Rosenthal and Ratzka, p. 17.

32. *Report of Commission* . . . , p. 5.

33. Ibid., p. 14.

34. Rosenthal and Ratzka, p. 176 and Kahn, unpublished manuscript, II, p. 36.

35. Henry-Russell Hitchcock, "Some American Interiors in the Modern Style," *Architectural Record*, 64 (Sept. 1928), 235.

36. Metropolitan Museum of Art, *The Architect and the Industrial Arts—An Exhibition of Contemporary American Design*, Feb. 12 to March 24 and continued to Sept. 2, 1929 (1929). See also Rosenthal and Ratzka, pp. 178-79; Kahn, manuscript, II, p. 32; and Arthur Tappan North, *Raymond Hood*, Contemporary American Architects series (New York: McGraw-Hill, 1931), p. 70.

37. Charles Rennie Mackintosh's work in Glasgow may also be seen as prefiguring the Art Deco style. However, his work does not seem to have the same continuity with the twenties that we can find in Hoffmann's architecture and the designs of the Wiener Werkstätte. Some of the more classicizing work of Joseph Olbrich at the Darmstadt Artists' Colony, such as the Ernst-Ludwig Haus and the entrance to the wedding tower, might also be included in a list of sources for Art Deco.

38. *Die Wiener Werkstätte—Modernes Kunsthandwerk*, exhibition catalogue (Vienna, 1967), p. 13.

39. Rosenthal and Ratzka, p. 59.

40. Sheldon Cheney, *The New World Architecture* (London, New York, and Toronto: Longmans, Green & Co., 1930), pp. 25 and 186.

41. See Max Eisler, *Dagobert Peche* (Vienna and Leipzig: Gerlach & Widling, 1925). Peche designed black-and-white-striped furniture as early as 1915. Striped furniture in starkly contrasting colors became a fad in the twenties (Veronesi claims that such designs in Art Deco derive from designs by Leon Bakst made between 1919 and 1923; p. 42).

42. Rosenthal and Ratzka, p. 173. According to these authors Wiener Werkstätte products, together with silks by Paul Poiret (p. 42), had been imported by John Wanamaker's as early as 1913.

43. Leon V. Solon, "The Viennese Method for Artistic Display—New York Galleries of the Wiener Werkstätte," *Architectural Record* 53 (March 1923), 266-71.

44. Solon, p. 266.

45. Frankl, *New Dimensions*, p. 76.

46. Kahn, manuscript, II, p. 31.

47. Egerton Swartwout, "Review of Recent Architectural Magazines," *American Architect*, 127 (March 15, 1925), 279.

48. However, some of the more fantastic designs of this period, Mies' and Poelzig's skyscraper projects, had been illustrated in Walter Curt Behrendt's article "Skyscrapers in Germany," *Journal of the American Institute of Architects*, 11 (Sept. 1923), 365-70.

49. Fiske Kimball, *American Architecture* (Indianapolis & New York: Bobbs-Merrill, 1928), p. 209.

50. *American Architect*, 127 (March 15, 1925), 281. The illustrations of the Chilehaus and the Ballinhaus were taken from *Moderne Bauformen*. The Chilehaus was illustrated again in the same year in "Gleaned from the

Foreign Architectural Press," *American Architect*, 128 (1925), 551-52. The Chilehaus was also illustrated in Frankl's *New Dimensions*. For further illustrations of German Expressionist architecture see also Wolfgang Pehnt, *Expressionist Architecture* (New York and Washington: Praeger, 1973), Eng. trans. by J. A. Underwood and Edith Küstner.

51. Triangular piers had also been used by Bruno Taut in a series of buildings designed for Magdeburg. Earlier American Neogothic skyscrapers, such as Cass Gilbert's Woolworth Building of 1913, had also used such piers. In this instance it is, therefore, difficult to say whether their use in Art Deco derives from American Neogothic architecture or from German Gothicizing Expressionist architecture, or both.

In the case of Voorhees, Gmelin & Walker, the German influence can be clearly established because of Gmelin's German background. The firm's library contained many books on contemporary German architecture, as well as a collection on German and American stage and cinema design. Among them: Eric Mendelsohn, *Amerika* (Berlin, 1926); Hermann Muthesius, *Die Schöne Wohnung* (Munich, 1922); Oliver Saylor, ed., *Max Reinhardt and his Theater* (New York, 1924); Paul Zucker, *Theater und Lichtspielhäuser* (Berlin, 1926); Fr. Kranich, *Bühnentechnik der Gegenwart* (Munich and Berlin, 1929); Günther Herkt, *Das Tonfilm Theater* (Berlin, 1931); Joseph Urban, *Theaters* (New York, 1929); Kenneth MacGowan and Robert Edmond Jones, *Continental Stagecraft* (New York, 1922); Sheldon Cheney, *The Art Theater* (New York, 1917); R. W. Sexton and B. F. Betts, *American Theatres of Today* (New York, 1927, 2 vols.); and many others.

A somewhat vaguer relationship between an American architect and a central European influence can be seen in Harvey Wiley Corbett's interest in Frederick Kiesler's designs. Kiesler, a Viennese-born architect who had been a member of the Berlin G group and the Dutch de Stijl movement before coming to America, in 1926 exhibited plans for his Endless House at the New York Theater Guild, where Corbett saw them and began taking an interest in Kiesler. According to Kiesler himself, he worked for two years in Corbett's architectural firm (Thomas H. Creighton interview with Kiesler, "Kiesler's Pursuit of an Idea," *Progressive Architecture*, 42 (July 1961), 105-16). However, Wallace K. Harrison claimed in a private interview that Kiesler never joined Corbett's office officially but that Corbett fostered Kiesler's career and took a special interest in Kiesler's design for the Eighth Street Playhouse (1929; today much altered), which seems to owe a debt to Mendelsohn's Universum Theater in Berlin.

52. This goal is explicitly stated by Behrens himself in his opening speech of the exhibition, "Die Dombauhütte," *Deutsche Kunst und Dekoration*, 26 (Jan. 1923), 221-30.

53. Peter Behrens "Administration Buildings for Industrial Plants," *American Architect*, 128 (August 1925), 167-74. This essay contains an illustration of the I. G. Farben main hall. See also Peter Behrens, "Seeking Aesthetic worth in Industrial Buildings" (transl. by Arthur Woltersdorf) *American Architect*, 128 (Dec. 5, 1925), 475-79. This essay deals primarily with Hans Poelzig's and Behrens' own work and contains, among others, an illustration of a brick office building by Hans Poelzig in Hanover with a dominant zigzag motif. Behrens' work was again extensively illustrated in Shepard Vogelgesang, "Peter Behrens, Architect and Teacher," *The Architectural Forum*, 52 (May 1930), 715-21. The much more idiosyncratic brick Expressionism of Bernhard Hoetger—as, for example, in his Paula Modersohn-Becker House of 1926—did not seem to receive the same publicity here as the work of

Behrens, Poelzig, or Höger. However, the brick detailing over the entrance to the RCA Victor Building is perhaps comparable to some of the sculptural brick surfaces of the Modersohn-Becker House.

54. Saarinen's station was published in the States after his *succès d'estime* with his Tribune Tower competition design of 1922 and arrival in America the following year (see Albert Christ-Janer, *Eliel Saarinen*, foreword by Alvar Aalto [Chicago: University of Chicago Press, 1948], p. 132).

55. F. R. Yerbury, ed., *Modern Dutch Buildings* (London: Ernest Benn, 1931). This gives a good overview of Dutch work considered important in the early thirties. Suzanne Frank's unpublished dissertation, "Michel de Klerk (1884-1923)—An Architect of the Amsterdam School" (Columbia University, 1969), contains useful information on Van der Meij's Scheepvaarthuis.

56. Clarence Stein, "Amsterdam, Old and New," *Journal of the American Institute of Architects*, 10 (October 1922), 310-28, and F. C. Brown, "De Dageraad," *Architectural Record*, 57 (Jan. 1925), 72-73. See also Edith Elmer Wood, "Recent Housing in the Netherlands," *Architectural Record*, 53 (Feb. 1923), 173.

57. Editorial, "Some Buildings in a Dutch Housing Community—W. M. Dudok, Architect," *Architectual Forum*, 38 (May 1923), 235-38.

58. Cheney, p. 29.

59. In books on Art Deco crafts the vibrant colors that became fashionable in the twenties are usually ascribed to the influence of Leon Bakst's stage and costume design for Diaghilev's Russian Ballet. However, we should remember that the French Fauves and the German Expressionists had utilized bright colors before Bakst. Bakst should be seen in this context as a popularizer, not an originator.

60. Bruno Taut in his postwar utopian books frequently proposed the use of color shading in architecture, where the color becomes lighter toward the top of the building, a device applied by Behrens in the I. G. Farben main hall (mentioned earlier) and used in the later twenties in several brick buildings in New York. Taut's work was probably known to American readers. For example, Taut's Glass House for the Cologne *Werkbund* Exposition of 1914 was illustrated in the context of a discussion on glass products (Editorial, "Glass as a Decorative and Structural Product," *American Architect*, 132 (Oct. 5, 1927), 456); Ely Jacques Kahn also seems to have been familiar with Taut's work (Ely Jacques Kahn, "Sources of Inspiration," *Architecture*, 60 (Nov. 1929), 251); and Talbot Hamlin refers to Taut as an architect distinct from the International Style movement and praises Taut's book *Modern Architecture* of 1929 (see Talbot Faulkner Hamlin, "The International Style Lacks the Essence of Great Architecture," *American Architect*, 143 (Jan. 1933), 12).

62. Leon Solon, "Principles of Architectural Polychromy," *Architectural Record*, 51, (1922), 1-7, 93-100, 189-96, 285-91, 377-86, 465-75.

62. Leon Solon, *Polychromy* (New York: Architectural Record, 1924).

63. Alfred C. Bossom, "Nicholas Roerich," *Architectural Record*, 50 (Aug. 1921), 83.

64. C. Howard Walker, "Architectural Polychromy," *Architectural Record*, 53 (March 1923), 272-78.

65. W. Francklyn Paris, "The International Exposition of Modern Industrial and Decorative Art in Paris," *Architectural Record*, 58 (Oct. 1925), 365-85.

66. Ely Jacques Kahn, "On Decoration and Ornament," in Arthur Tappan North, *Ely Jacques Kahn* Contemporary American Architects Series (New York: McGraw-Hill, 1931), pp. 21 and 24.

67. North, *Raymond Hood*, p. 14. Henry-Russell Hitchcock wrote in 1932 that

Hood's polychrome façade for the Patterson House at Ossining was suggestive of the "fantasies of the German expressionists" (Museum of Modern Art, *Modern Architecture*, p. 130).

68. Sheldon Cheney, *Expressionism in Art* (New York: Liveright, 1934), p. 378.

69. Roi L. Morin, "Design and Construction of Theaters—Part V—The Auditorium," *American Architect*, 123 Jan. 1923), 57-58, 66-67.

70. Indirect lighting and nighttime illumination of buildings had become widespread by the time of the 1925 Paris exhibition (see particularly the Polish Pavilion by Joseph Czajkowski, which had a glass superstructure that was illuminated at night).

71. Kenneth Macgowan, *The Theatre of Tomorrow* (New York: Boni & Liveright, 1921).

72. Herbert Kroly, "New Dimensions in Architectural Effects," *Architectural Record*, 57 (Jan. 1925), 94.

73. Harvey Wiley Corbett, "Design in Office Buildings," *The Architectural Forum*, 52 (June 1930), 779.

74. Kahn, "On the Use of Color," Arthur Tappan North, *Ely Jacques Kahn*, p. 24.

75. Leon Solon, "Will the Exposition Regain Artistic Leadership for France?" *Architectural Record*, 58 (Oct. 1925), 391-93. Alfred Bossom in "The Rebirth of Art and Architecture in Europe," expressed a counterview "European art and architecture are being reborn on the banks of the Seine. The Exposition . . . has been compared to the Italian Renaissance." (*American Architect*, 128 [Aug. 26, 1925], 161).

76. Leo Friedlander, "The New Architecture and the Master Sculptor," *The Architectural Forum*, 46 (Jan. 1927), 1.

77. Ely Jacques Kahn, "The Province of Decoration in Modern Design," *Creative Art*, 5 (Dec. 1929), 885.

78. Fiske Kimball, *American Architecture* (Indianapolis and New York: Bobbs-Merrill, p. 210.

79. Cheney, *The New World Architecture*, pp. 29 and 175.

80. Park refers to veneers of thin walls hung over skeleton frames (p. 151) and to walls that are merely curtains hung on a great frame (p. 126). W. A. Starrett, *Skyscrapers and the Men Who Build Them* (New York and London: Charles Scribner's Sons, 1928), mentions "curtain walls" specificially (caption for illustration opposite page 222).

81. Godfried [sic] Semper, "Development of Architectural Style," transl. and arranged by John W. Root, *The Inland Architect and News Record*, 14 (Dec. 1889), 76-78; 14 (Jan. 1890), 92-94; 15 (Feb. 1890), 5-6; 15 (March 1890), 32-33. Illinois State Association of Architects "Discussion," *The Inland Architect and News Record*, 9 (March 1887), 26. In an obituary for Semper (J. T. C., "Gottfried Semper," *The American Architect and Building News*, 7, part I, [Jan. 31, 1880], 36-37 and part II, [Feb. 7, 1880], 43-44) the importance of his *Der Stil* is pointed out and all of his essays published in foreign periodicals known to the author are listed.

82. Semper discusses this in his essay *Die vier Elemente der Baukunst* (Braunschweig, 1851).

83. Semper's importance for Sullivan was pointed out in the twenties by Fiske Kimball in "Louis Sullivan—An Old Master," *Architectural Record*, 57 (April 1925), 289-304.

84. Wright's works of this period were discussed in the following essays, among others: Louis H. Sullivan, "Concerning the Imperial Hotel, Tokyo, Japan," *Architectural Record*, 53 (April 1923), 332-52; A. N. Rebori, "Frank Lloyd Wright's Textile-Block Slab Construction," *Architectural Record*, 62 (Dec. 1927), 449-56; and Douglas Haskell, "Organic Architecture: Frank Lloyd

Wright," *Creative Art*, 3 (Nov. 1928), Ii-Ivii. Wright himself published a series of essays, "In the Cause of Architecture," in the *Architectural Record* of 1928 (vol. 63, pp. 49-57, 145-51, 350-56, 481-88, and 555-61).

85. The *Architectural Record* did publish a well-illustrated article on Mayan architecture by S. K. Lothrop, "The Architecture of the Ancient Mayas," (57 [April 1925], 491-509). However, the essay seems purely archaeological; there is never any intention of this style's application for contemporary architecture.

86. Hillier in *The World of Art Deco*, pp. 26-32, develops an elaborate theory that American architects may have identified with the political situation in Mexico and, therefore, imitated Mexico's architecture. We have found no evidence for this, at least in New York. The stepped design of many Art Deco crafts is often referred to as "Aztec." Paul Frankl, however, calls his stepped pieces of furniture "skyscraper furniture"; crafts design in this instance, in other words, was imitating skyscraper design under the set-back law, not Aztec forms. If architects in New York ever had in mind Pre-Columbian architecture, it came as an afterthought.

87. Rose Henderson, "A Primitive Basis for Modern Architecture," *Architectural Record*, 54 (August 1923), 189.

88. See Frankl, *New Dimensions*, p. 45.

89. See Park, p. 141 and ill. 62.

90. Editorial, "Current News—Motion Picture Producers Recognize Efforts of Architects in the Productions," *American Architect*, 117 (Feb. 4, 1920), p. 157.

91. Ben J. Lubschez, "The Cabinet of Dr. Caligari," *Journal of the American Institute of Architects*, 9 (Jan. 1921), 213-16. The importance of *Caligari* as well as *The Golem* is also discussed in Macgowan, *The Theatre of Tomorrow*, p. 119.

92. Rosenthal and Ratzka, pp. 170-71. They also mention the great impact *Caligari* had.

93. *Architectural Record*, 52 (1922), 170.

94. Lewis Jacobs, *The Rise of the American Film* (New York: Teachers College Press, 1968), p. 303.

95. Frank Vreeland, "Worth While Pictures of the Month," *Theatre Magazine*, 36 (Sept. 1921), 175.

96. Hillier, *Art Deco*, p. 37.

97. P[eter] Bogdanovich, *Fritz Lang in America* (New York: Praeger, 1967), p. 15. At the American opening of *Metropolis* in 1927 10,000 people queued up in front of the Rialto Theater (Paul M. Jensen, *The Cinema of Fritz Lang* [New York: A. S. Barnes, 1969], p. 58).

98. Rosenthal and Ratzka, p. 175.

99. Cheney, *The New World Architecture*, p. 120.

100. Park, p. 41.

101. Frankl, *New Dimensions*, p. 16.

102. Ibid.

103. Frankl, *Form and Re-Form*, pp. 3, 5.

104. Park, p. 77.

105. Frankl, *Form and Re-Form*, p. 163.

106. Ibid., p. 165.

107. See Klaus-Jürgen Sembach, *Style 1930* (New York: Universe Books, 1971), and Sheldon and Martha Cheney, *Art and the Machine* (New York: Whittlesey House, 1936).

108. Cheney, *The New World Architecture*, 75.

109. Norman Bel Geddes, *Horizons* (Boston: Little, Brown & Co., 1932). But see Clement Edson Armi, "The Formation of the Torpedo Tourer," *Society of*

Architectural Historians Journal, 29 (Dec. 1970), 339-46. He shows that racing cars and "future cars" had applied streamlining from about 1910 onward, affecting even the design of commercial vehicles to some extent. Only the very obvious airflow shapes characteristic of the thirties seem to be new.

110. Oskar Beyer, ed., *Eric Mendelsohn: Letters of an Architect*, introduction by Nikolaus Pevsner, transl. by Geoffrey Strachan (London, New York, Toronto: Abelard-Schuman, 1967), pp. 71-74.

111. A[lfred] H. B[arr], Jr., Foreword, *Machine Art*, Museum of Modern Art, N.Y., March 6–April 30, 1934, unpaged.

112. Elizabeth Mock, Foreword, *Built in USA—1932-1944*, Museum of Modern Art, N.Y., 1944, p. 12.

113. Talbot Hamlin, "The International Style Lacks the Essence of Great Architecture." *The American Architect*, 143 (Jan. 1933), 12.

114. Ibid., p. 16.

115. Howard McKee, "*Frank Lloyd Wright and the Chicago World's Fair of 1933*," unpublished paper, Avery Library, Columbia University, 1964, p. 12. Wright's Town Hall lecture took place in 1931.

116. Frank Lloyd Wright, *An Autobiography* (New York: Duell, Sloan and Pearce, 1943), p. 353.

A SELECTED LIST

of 115 Art Deco buildings in New York City
including the major buildings
and representative examples of minor building types

Buildings 13, 17, 23, 29, 30, 33, 37, 38, 41, 47, 52, 48, 62, 78, 79, 84, 91, and 111 are not illustrated. Buildings marked with an asterisk are illustrated wholly or partly in the color section following p. 40.

1923

1. Barclay-Vesey Building. McKenzie, Voorhees & Gmelin, 1923-26. Barclay, Vesey, Washington, and West Streets.

1925

2. Cheney Brothers Store. Ferrobrandt and Howard Greenley, 1925. Madison Avenue at 34th Street.

1926

3. Insurance Center Building. Buchman & Kahn, 1926-27. John, Platt, and Gold Streets.
4. *The Lowell. Henry S. Churchill and Herbert Lippmann, 1926. 63rd Street between Park and Madison.
5. 420 Madison Avenue. Dennison & Hirons, 1926-27. Between 48th and 49th Streets.

1927

6. *Park Avenue Building. Buchman & Kahn, 1927. At 32nd and 33rd Streets.
7. *42 West 39th Street. Buchman & Kahn 1927. Between Fifth and Sixth Avenues.
8. Panhellenic Tower. John Mead Howells, 1927-30. First Avenue just east of 49th Street.

9. *Chanin Building. Sloan & Robertson, 1927-30. Lexington Avenue at 41st and 42nd Streets.
10. Manufacturers Trust Branch, Eighth Avenue and 43rd Street. Dennison & Hirons, 1927-28?
11. International Magazine Company Building. Joseph Urban, 1927-28. Eighth Avenue at 56th and 57th Streets.

1928

12. Beaux-Arts Institute of Design. Dennison & Hirons, 1928. 44th Street between First and Second Avenues.
13. Fort Wadsworth Towers. H. I. Feldman, 1928. West 188th Street and Wadsworth Terrace.
14. Apartments, 3 East 84th Street. Howells & Hood, 1928. Off Fifth Avenue.
15. Apartments, 68th Street and Third Avenue. George & Edward Blum, 1928.
16. 275 Seventh Avenue, Buchman & Kahn 1928. At 25th and 26th Streets.
17. Apartments, 22nd Street and Second Avenue. George & Edward Blum, 1928.
18. Fuller Building. Walker & Gillette, 1928-29. 57th Street and Madison Avenue.
19. Master Building. Helmle, Corbett & Harrison and Sugarman & Berger, 1928-29. Riverside Drive and 103rd Street.
20. Apartments, Central Park West and 94th Street. Schwartz & Gross, 1928-29.
21. 261 Fifth Avenue. Buchman & Kahn, 1928-29. At 29th Street.
22. Broadway Block Building. Schultze & Weaver, 1928-29. At Broadway and 51st and 52nd Streets.
23. Allied Arts Building. Buchman & Kahn, 1928-29. 45th Street between First and Second Avenues.
24. *Film Center Building. Buchman & Kahn, 1928-29. Ninth Avenue at 44th and 45th Streets.
25. Stewart & Company (later Bonwit Teller) Store. Warren & Wetmore (altered by Ely Jacques Kahn), 1928-30. Fifth Avenue at 56th Street.
26. *Chrysler Building. William Van Alen, 1928-30. Lexington Avenue at 42nd and 43rd Streets.
27. Western Union Building. Voorhees, Gmelin & Walker, 1928-30. Hudson, Thomas, and Worth Streets and West Broadway.
28. The Navarre. Sugarman & Berger, 1928-30. Seventh Avenue and 38th Street.

1929

29. Horn & Hardart, Sixth Avenue and 45th Street. F. P. Platt & Brother, 1929.
30. Apartments, 68th Street and Second Avenue. George & Edward Blum, 1929?
31. Wadsworth Manor. H. I. Feldman, 1929. Wadsworth Terrace at 190th Street.

32. Apartments, 240 East 79th Street. Godwin, Thompson & Patterson, 1929. Between Second and Third Avenues.

33. Corn Exchange Branch. Fellheimer & Wagner, 1929. St. Nicholas Avenue between 167th and 168th Streets.

34. Office building, 501 Madison Avenue. Robert D. Kohn and Frank Vitolo, 1929-30. At 52nd Street.

35. *News Building. Howells & Hood, 1929-30. 42nd and 41st Streets and Second Avenue.

36. Salvation Army Building. Voorhees, Gmelin & Walker, 1929-30. 13th and 14th Streets between Sixth and Seventh Avenues.

37. Downtown Athletic Club. Starrett & Van Vleck, 1929-30. West and Washington Streets between Morris Street and Battery Place.

38. Apartments, Park Avenue and 79th Street. Sloan & Robertson, 1929-30.

39. The Eldorado. Margon & Holder, 1929-30. Central Park West at 90th and 91st Streets.

40: Squibb Building. Buchman & Kahn, 1929-30. Fifth Avenue at 58th Street.

41. Bricken-Continental Building, Buchman & Kahn 1929-30. Broadway, Seventh Avenue, and 41st Street.

42. Essex House. Frank Grad, 1929-30. Central Park South between Sixth and Seventh Avenues.

43. Kent Columbus Circle Garage. Jardine, Hill & Murdock, 1929-30. Columbus Avenue and 61st Street.

44. Telephone Building, East 13th Street. Voorhees, Gmelin & Walker, 1929-30. On Second Avenue.

45. Telephone Building, West 17th and 18th Streets. Voorhees, Gmelin & Walker, 1929-30. Between Seventh and Eighth Avenues.

46. Telephone Building, West 50th Street. Voorhees, Gmelin & Walker, 1929-30. Between Ninth and Tenth Avenues.

47. Hollywood Theater. T. W. Lamb, 1929-30. 51st Street between Broadway and Eighth Avenue.

48. Beaux-Arts Apartment Hotel. Murchison & Hood, Godley & Fouilhoux, 1929-30. 44th Street between First and Second Avenues.

49. Barbizon Plaza. Murgatroyd & Ogden, 1929-30. Central Park South, 58th Street, and Sixth Avenue.

50. National Title Guaranty Company. Corbett, Harrison & MacMurray, 1929-30. Montague Street between Clinton Street and Cadman Plaza, Brooklyn.

51. New School for Social Research. Joseph Urban, 1929-30. 12th Street between Fifth and Sixth Avenues.

52. City Bank Farmers Trust Building. Cross & Cross 1929-31. William, Hanover, and Beaver Streets and Exchange Place.

53. Southgate Apartments. Emery Roth, 1929-31. 52nd Street east of First Avenue.

54. Irving Trust Building. Voorhees, Gmelin & Walker, 1929-32. Wall and New Streets and Broadway.

55. House of Detention for Women. Sloan & Robertson, 1929-32. Sixth and Greenwich Avenues and 10th Street (demolished).

56. Bloomingdale's on Lexington Avenue. Starrett & Van Vleck, 1930. At 59th and 60th Streets.

57. *The Town House. Bowden & Russell, 1930. 38th Street between Lexington and Park Avenues.

58. 21 West Street. Starrett & Van Vleck, 1930. Morris and Washington Streets.

59. Curb Exchange façade. Starrett & Van Vleck, 1930. Trinity Place between Thames and Rector Streets.

60. *Twentieth-Century Fox Building. Joseph J. Furman, 1930. 56th Street between Ninth and Tenth Avenues.

61. West Side Elevated Highway. Architectural design by John Sloan, 1930. Between Canal Street and Riverside Park.

62. Hotel Carlyle. Bien & Prince, 1930. Madison Avenue at 76th and 77th Streets.

63. Office tower, southeast corner 40th Street and Madison Avenue. Kenneth Franzheim, 1930.

64. *Apartments, Central Park West at 66th Street. Schwartz & Gross, 1930.

65. New Amsterdam apartments. Margon & Holder, 1930. 86th Street and Amsterdam Avenue.

66. Apartments, Central Park West and 84th Street. Schwartz & Gross, 1930.

67. Apartments, 40 West 86th Street. J. M. Felson, 1930-31. Between Central Park West and Columbus Avenue.

68. The Ardsley. Emery Roth, 1930-31. Central Park West and 92nd Street.

69. Horn & Hardart, 33rd Street. Louis Allen Abramson, 1930-31. Between Seventh Avenue and Greeley Square.

70. *Horn & Hardart, 181st Street. Louis Allen Abramson, 1930-31. Between Wadsworth and St. Nicholas Avenues.

71. RCA Victor Building. Cross & Cross, 1930-31. Lexington Avenue and 51st Street.

72. Sears Roebuck Building. Frank S. Parker, 1930-31. Ninth Avenue and 31st Street.

73. American Savings Bank, 42nd Street. Hirons & Mellor, 1930-31. Between Sixth Avenue and Times Square.

74. Waldorf-Astoria. Schultze & Weaver, 1930-31. Park and Lexington Avenues and 49th and 50th Streets.

75. 500 Fifth Avenue. Shreve, Lamb & Harmon 1930-31. At 42nd Street.

76. Empire State Building. Shreve, Lamb & Harmon, 1930-31. Fifth Avenue and 33rd and 34th Streets.

77. 29 Broadway. Sloan & Robertson, 1930-31. Morris Street and Trinity Place.

78. Newsweek Building. Robert D. Kohn, 1930-31. 49th and 50th Streets and Madison Avenue.

79. Hotel Edison. H. J. Knapp, 1930-31. 47th Street between Duffy Square and Eighth Avenue.

80. Bricken-Casino Building. Firm of Ely Jacques Kahn, 1930-31. Broadway and 39th Street.

81. 1400 Broadway. Buchman & Kahn, 1930-31. 38th and 39th Streets.
82. *McGraw-Hill Building. Hood, Godley & Fouilhoux, 1930-31. 42nd and 41st Streets between Eighth and Ninth Avenues.
83. Broadway Fashion Building. Sugarman & Berger, 1930-31. Broadway at 84th Street.
84. Daily Commerce Building. Buchman & Kahn, 1930-31. 44th Street and Third Avenue.
85. 60 Wall Tower. Clinton & Russell, Holton & George, 1930-32. Pine, Pearl, and Cedar Streets.
86. Northeast corner 45th Street and Lexington Avenue. F. R. Stuckert, 1930-32.

1931

87. Majestic Apartments. Office of Irwin S. Chanin, 1931. Central Park West and 71st and 72nd Streets.
88. Earl Carroll Theater. George Keister, 1931. Seventh Avenue at 50th Street.
89. Long Island Area Headquarters, New York Telephone Company. Voorhees, Gmelin & Walker, 1931. Bridge and Willoughby Streets, Brooklyn.
90. RCA Building. Associated Architects, 1931-33. Rockefeller Plaza and 49th and 50th Streets.
91. Americas Building. Associated Architects, 1931-32. Sixth Avenue and 51st Street.
92. Radio City Music Hall. Associated Architects, 1931-32. Sixth Avenue and 50th Street.
93. Fourth Church of Christ Scientist. Cherry & Matz, 1931-32. Ft. Washington Avenue and 185th Street.
94. Metropolitan Life, North Building. H. W. Corbett and D. E. Waide, 1931-33. Park Avenue, Madison Square, and 24th and 25th Streets.

1932

95. Provident Loan Society Branch, 72nd Street. Renwick, Aspinwall & Guard, 1932. Between Amsterdam and Columbus Avenues (demolished).
96. Century Apartments. Office of Irwin S. Chanin, 1932. Central Park West and 62nd and 63rd Streets.
97. British Empire Building and Maison Française. Associated Architects, 1932-33. Fifth Avenue and 49th and 50th Streets.
98. City of New York Central Substation. 1932. 53rd Street between Sixth and Seventh Avenues.
99. City of New York Greenwich Substation. 1932. West 13th Street and Greenwich Avenue.

1933

100. Midtown Theater. Boak & Paris, 1933. Broadway between 99th and 100th Streets.

101. Federal Office Building. Cross & Cross, 1933-35. Vesey, Church, and Barclay Streets and West Broadway.
102. Palazzo d'Italia. Associated Architects, 1933-35. Fifth Avenue and 50th Street.
103. International Buildings. Associated Architects, 1933-35. Fifth Avenue and 50th and 51st Streets.
104. City of New York Smith Street Substation. 1933. Second Place and Smith Street, South Brooklyn.

1934

105. East River Savings Bank. Walker & Gillette, 1934-35. Trinity Place and Cortlandt and Dey Streets.

1935

106. Kress Building. Edward F. Sibbert, 1935. Fifth Avenue and 39th Street.
107. Piers 88, 90, and 92. 1935 (demolished).
108. Apartments, 80th Street and West End Avenue. George F. Pelham 2nd, 1935-36.

1936

109. Time & Life Building. Associated Architects, 1936-37. Rockefeller Plaza and 48th and 49th Streets.

1938

110. Horn & Hardart, 57th Street. Ralph B. Bencker, 1938. Between Sixth and Seventh Avenues.
111. Provident Loan Society Branch, 43rd Street. Renwick, Aspinwall & Guard, 1938. Between Lexington and Third Avenues.

1939

112. Criminal Courts Building. H. W. Corbett, 1939. Center, White, Baxter, and Leonard Streets.
113. Joan of Arc Junior High School. Eric Kebbon, 1939-40. 92nd and 93rd Streets between Columbus and Amsterdam Avenues.
114. Airlines Building. John B. Peterkin, 1939-40. 42nd and 41st Streets and Park Avenue.
115. Tiffany Building. Cross & Cross, 1939-40. Fifth Avenue and 57th Street.

PLATES

1. BARCLAY-VESEY BUILDING

A. This building just north of the Trade Center towers was one of a great number built by telephone companies throughout the country in the 1920s. Bell System policy seems to have called consistently for progressive design; this building by McKenzie, Voorhees & Gmelin was the first in the Art Deco style. Housing both equipment and corporate offices, it stood out as the largest telephone building in the world, and to contemporary architects was remarkable also in having—as it seemed to them—neither in its massing nor in its decorative detail any trace of an historical style. A photograph of it served as frontispiece to English-language editions of Le Corbusier's *Towards a New Architecture*. The lot is in the shape of a parallelogram; the tower is square. Hence the twist between the base of the building and the tower.

B. Aborigines and the company's bell appear among plant forms above the entrances.

C. Exotic animals and plants are carved on the arches of the building's arcade (originally a shopping arcade) and over the windows above.

D. The main lobby was described by Lewis Mumford as being "as gaily . . . decorated as a village street in a strawberry festival."

E. Elevator doors off the ground floor lobby are demonstrably hand-wrought.

F. Decorative relief is continued on a grill above the door of the board room on the executive level.

G. Decorative relief also appeared on the lintel of a door leading from an anteroom to the board room and on the plaster coving above it. The coving is remarkable in evidently being German Expressionist in origin.

H and I. Within the boardroom, the furniture, such as the table shown here, is in a vertical arts and crafts style—vertical as in some of the "skyscraper" furniture of the period.

2. CHENEY BROTHERS STORE

A and B. The French ironworker Edgar Brandt established a New York branch called Ferrobrandt under the direction of Jules Bouy. These gates were made by Ferrobrandt for a silk store of 1925 on Madison Avenue cater-cornered from Altman's.

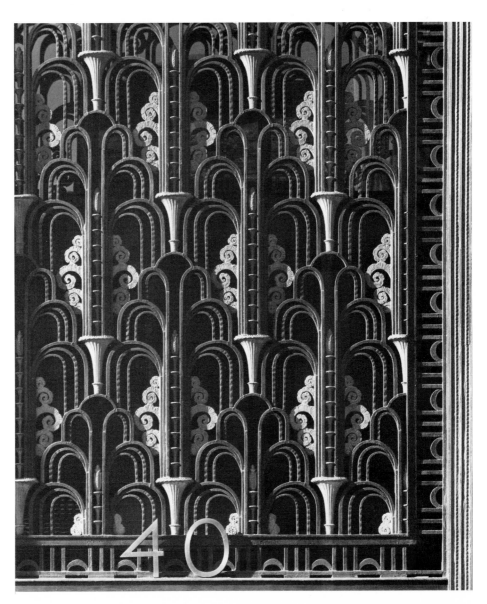

C. The building in which Cheney Brothers had their ground-floor shop, the Madison-Belmont by Warren & Wetmore, also had an entrance screen by Ferrobrandt.

3. INSURANCE CENTER BUILDING

A form of zigzag which became a common feature of New York Art Deco buildings first appears on this one of 1926, designed by Buchman & Kahn for the district just to the north of Wall Street. This zigzag probably comes ultimately from textile sources as did (according to the designer, Ely Jacques Kahn) the design of the cornice of the slightly earlier Furniture Exchange Building (on Lexington Avenue between 32nd and 33rd Streets; see p. 15). The Insurance Center Building was the first of a cluster of Kahn buildings in Downtown Manhattan which would eventually surround and largely hide this first one.

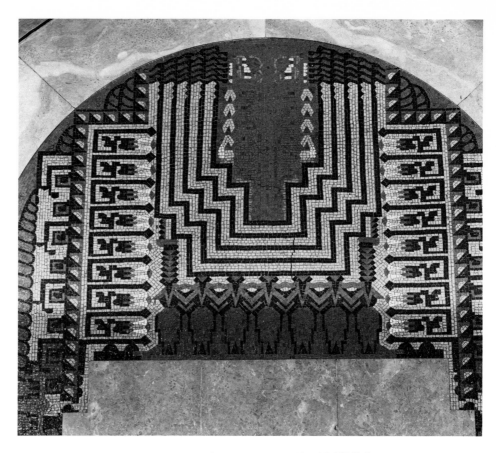

6. THE PARK AVENUE BUILDING

B. The masterpiece of the New York Art Deco, Ely Kahn's office building of 1927 for the lower end of Park Avenue, has towards its top glazed terra-cotta cladding whose colors were carefully designed to be effective from a distance (see exterior view in color section). In the lobby original mosaics are still in place, but the original lamps and the main ceiling decoration are no more. Lewis Mumford wrote of the building: "One swallow may not make a summer; but one building like this, which faces the entire problem of design, and has a clean, unflinching answer for each question, may well serve to crystallize all the fumbling and uncertain elements in present-day architecture."

5. 420 MADISON

Flat fields of curvilinear ornament, a characteristic of architectural design at the 1925 Paris show, made their appearance in New York on this small office building on Madison Avenue by Dennison & Hirons, built in 1926-27.

B. Decorative terra-cotta panels were by René Chambellan. The building, erected in 1927-28, is a short distance north of the UN Building.

8. PANHELLENIC HOTEL

A. John Mead Howells' orange brick and terra-cotta tower was one of a number of buildings, including the Barclay-Vesey Building and Raymond Hood's earlier American Radiator Building, which looked to Eliel Sarrinen's Chicago Tribune entry as a pattern for the style-less skyscraper.

9. CHANIN BUILDING

A. This office tower of 1927-30 at 42nd Street and Lexington Avenue near Grand Central was built by and for the Chanin Brothers' construction firm and still contains its headquarters. Sloan & Robertson were the architects. Their style-less inspiration was again Saarinen's Tribune tower—the top of the Chanin appears in plate 57 in the color section, to the left of the Chrysler Building (26) and the Town House. Though it had more floors than the Woolworth, the world's tallest building at the time the Chanin was designed, the latter was not as tall.

B. A flat band of plant forms in terra-cotta appears three floors above street level. The building immediately to the right is Shreve, Lamb & Harmon's 500 Fifth Avenue (75).

C. Allegorical figures in the vestibules are by the sculptor René Chambellan.

D. Brass radiator grills, ea with a different design, a set in the walls of the lob (as they are below the al gorical figures in the ves bules). Here, as on 4 Madison (5), spiralli forms predomina

E. This window onto the Chanin lobby was originally that of a Longchamps Restaurant. The fan-shaped details in flat decorative panels are perhaps an expressive version of Minoan or Egyptian decoration.

F. At the executive level, metal gates include machine forms, the outline of a violin, and, at the base, stacks of money. The dynamic forms of this gate are reminiscent of the expressive ornament of the nineteenth-century designer Christopher Dresser, as is much Art Deco design.

G. A private bathroom has coved lighting. Glass doors close off a bathtub with shower.

10. MANUFACTURER'S TRUST BANK

This branch bank a block west of Times Square was built in 1927-28 to designs of Dennison & Hirons. Floral panels are incorporated into a Classical framework. The characteristic Art Deco spiral forms predominate. In the panels which top the pilasters, one can also detect a lingering relationship to Ionic or Corinthian volutes.

11. INTERNATIONAL MAGAZINE
BUILDING

A block south of Columbus Circle, this building of 1927-28 was designed by the Austrian-born designer Joseph Urban, who handled the Art Deco style, ultimately German and Austrian in its sources, with more assurance than his younger American colleagues and seemed to have none of their urge to build high. As in the Manufacturer's Trust Bank (10), Art Deco motifs are superimposed on a Neoclassical style: zigzags appear on urns.

A. The design of this building, the headquarters of the Beaux-Arts educational system in America, was determined by a competition. The first, second, and third prize winners were Frederic C. Hirons, Harry Sternfeld of Philadelphia, and William Van Alen, each of whom as a student had also won the Paris Prize to the Ecole in Paris. The winning Hirons design was erected in 1928. The Art Deco pilaster capitals are of Near Eastern and Greek inspiration.

12. BEAUX-ARTS INSTITUTE OF DESIGN

B. Statues were to have been mounted above the blocks at the second-floor level.

A. This small apartment house just off Fifth Avenue was designed by Raymond Hood and built in 1928 for Colonel Patterson of the Daily News.

14. 3 EAST 84TH STREET

B. On it appear for the first time the recessed metal spandrels that were to be a feature of many Art Deco skyscrapers to come.

15. 210 EAST 68TH STREET

This was one of a number of large apartment houses designed by George & Edward Blum, buildings across whose façades bands of terra-cotta ornament were sparsely stretched to give some individuality to what were essentially anonymous buildings.

16. 275 SEVENTH AVENUE

This building of 1928 was one of many designed by Buchman & Kahn for New York's garment district. It was in the public lobbies of these buildings that exuberant inventiveness in design was given free rein—especially in their molded plaster ceilings.

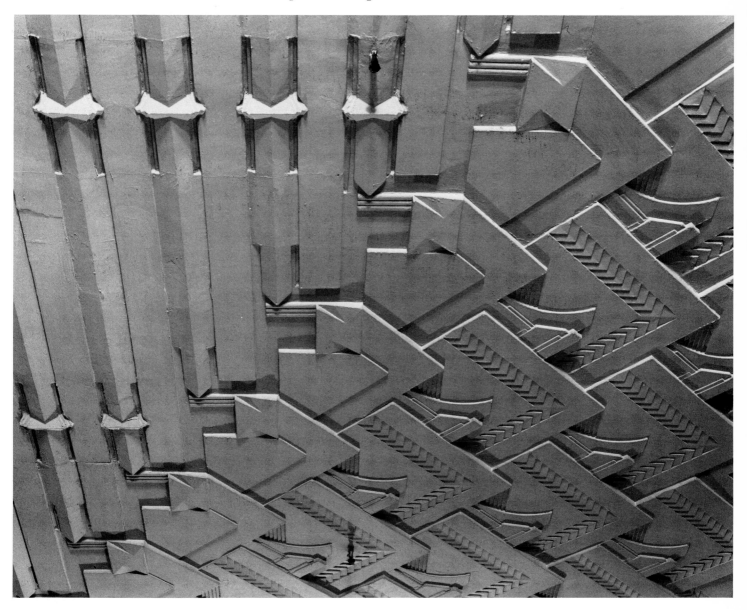

18. FULLER BUILDING

A. Like the Chanin (9), this building of 1928-29 on 57th Street was built for the headquarters of a construction firm (the Fuller Company's previous headquarters had been the Flatiron Building). The top is in black and white stone, which, with its forceful color contrast, has a primitive quality. The architects were Walker & Gillette. The building to the left is Ely Kahn's Squibb Building (40).

B. The entrance is surmounted by figures by Elie Nadelman which were added after 1931. Here too the ubiquitous Art Deco octagon is imposed on a clock.

19. MASTER BUILDING

A. This tower, the highest on Riverside Drive after the Riverside Church, was built in 1928-29 as a museum, art school, and apartment hotel combined. Designed by Helmle, Corbett & Harrison and Sugarman & Berger, it was one of a number of buildings of the twenties which had a curtain wall of brick shaded from a deep tone at the base to a lighter one at the building top. In this instance the base is in a dark purple brick which shades to a light grey at the crown. Inside, the museum space was innovative in being artificially lit. The Riverside Museum has now moved and the Master Institute of United Arts no longer exists. The Equity Theater is housed in what were the Institute's auditorium and the apartment hotel's restaurant.

B. The crowning motif is an early example of a faceted shape at a building's top, a device also used by Ely Kahn (see his Bricken-Casino building, 80). The faceted forms here, together with the shaded brick, suggest a German Expressionist influence.

A. This red brick and terra-cotta apartment tower of 1928-29 at 94th Street was the first of a series of apartment buildings that Schwartz & Gross designed for Central Park West addresses.

20. 336 CENTRAL PARK WEST

B. The terra-cotta cornices at the top of the building and its water tower housing seem to have been inspired by Egyptian precedents.

21. 261 FIFTH AVENUE

A. Forms appear at their most explicitly woven on the façade of this garment district loft building at 29th Street by Buchman & Kahn. It was built in 1928-29.

. Inside, the lobby still retains its molded plaster ceiling and, more surprisingly, its original lights.

22. BROADWAY BLOCK BUILDING

A. This small commercial building of 1928-29 on Broadway above Times
Square was designed by Schultze & Weaver, the architects who were to design the Waldorf-Astoria (74). On its façade irregular Art Deco octagons
serve as capitals for the pilasters. In the distance can be seen the Paramount
Building.

B. Construction began on the Paramount building in 1926 to designs of C. W. & George L. Rapp of Chicago in a style which was not Art Deco. Before completion the architects (or their clients) had been converted, and they added a clock tower surmounted by an illuminated glass ball; it is only these parts of this building that are in the style.

24. FILM CENTER BUILDING

B. This building of 1928-29 by Ely Jacques Kahn is on Ninth Avenue west of Times Square. It was designed to house a variety of activities which involve the handling of motion picture film. The forms of molded plaster and stone on the wall and ceiling of this vestibule and of the brass radiator grill below derive from fabric design. (For a view of the lobby beyond see the color section.)

A. This building of 1928-30 was no sooner finished to designs of [W]arren & Wetmore than it passed into the hands of Bonwit Teller and was remodeled for them by Ely Kahn. His contribution in[cl]uded the replacement of exuber[a]nt metal screens at the entrances with the more restrained ones that are still in place there.

25. STEWART & COMPANY STORE

B. At the top of the Fifth Avenue façade he left the chic figures and the urns above them intact.

26. CHRYSLER BUILDING

D. At its completion this building of 1928-30 by William Van Alen was the tallest in the world. The cresting at its top now contains radio transmitting equipment. E. In the tower below the spire, the topmost enclosed story originally formed an observation floor. Below that was a private luncheon club, the Cloud Club (still there; see below), and its gymnasia; a duplex apartment for Walter Chrysler, who had built the building; and early offices of Time, Inc.

F. At the base of the tower proper the building is pinched out at its corners and widens to a service floor at the 30th story, where there is a frieze of automobile hub caps and mudguards and, at the corners, winged radiator caps. The widening was meant to overcome an optical illusion from which the towers of horizontally striped towers were found to suffer: their tops appeared larger than their bases. Raymond Hood also took measures to overcome the illusion in his News Building (35) to the right, even though it did not have horizontal stripes—its terminal screen is curved in perceptibly.

G. Lower on the building, curtain walls have what was described at the time as the form of a basket-weave.

I. The entrance screen on the west side of the building still retains its crenel-lated band but lacks the black glass it once held as well as the original variety of textured glass above.

H. Entrances at ground level are in the form of proscenia and contain glass and metal screens.

J. The lobby is triangular in shape (see plan, p. 22) and, at exits and above the elevator lobbies, has coved cold-cathode lighting in the form of raised curtains.

K. The ceiling mural is by Edward Trumbull. The lines shown here were said to represent natural forces.

N. The main dining room of the Cloud Club towards the top of the building has lost its original furniture but is otherwise intact.

M. Staircases, which give access to the second floor and to the basement, are topped with ceilings finished in aluminum leaf.

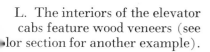

L. The interiors of the elevator cabs feature wood veneers (see color section for another example).

27. WESTERN UNION BUILDING

B. The mass of the building, in shaded orange brick and with a variety of chevrons in its decorative brickwork, forms an effective terminal to the view up West Broadway from above the new Trade Center towers.

A. The entrance to this building of 1928-30 by Voorhees, Gmelin & Walker is of brick, bronze, and glass and in proscenium form. The use of brick above the doorway in a textured and idiosyncratic fashion probably derives from German Expressionist and Dutch sources.

28. THE NAVARRE

This building of 1928-30 by Sugarman & Berger in the garment district south of Times Square has one entrance to its elevator lobby and a second entrance which originally led to a second-floor banking room (now an Off-Track Betting office).

31. WADSWORTH MANOR

A and B. This is a virtuoso brick and terra-cotta building of 1929 on Washington Heights by H. I. Feldman. Many modest apartment buildings followed the same course in the years to come. The triangular piers here, often used at this time, can be found earlier in Neogothic buildings and in German Expressionist brick buildings.

32. 240 EAST 79TH STREET

Godwin, Thompson & Patterson followed the example of the Lowell (4) in making a stage set in glazed terra-cotta of the ground floor of this East Side apartment house of 1929.

34. 501 MADISON AVENUE

detail of the building by Robert D. Kohn and Frank E. Vitolo is shown. Kohn was the architect of the Newsweek Building and of the extensions which carried the older Macy's Store of De Lemos & Cordes to Seventh Avenue. 501 Madison was built in 1929-30.

B and C. Raymond M. Hood's building of 1929-30 escaped the standard formula for twenties skyscrapers of a tower set on a ziggurat by taking the area of tower the zoning law allowed in a form approaching that of a slab.

35. THE NEWS BUILDING

D and E. At ground level there is a wealth of decoration, particularly in bronze. (See color section also.)

35E.

F. Inside, the lobby has been much altered in the building's enlargement in the fifties by Harrison & Abramovitz, but the globe which was at its center remains, as does the black glass ceiling over it, shown here.

A. This complex, designed by Voorhees, Gmelin & Walker and built in 1929-30, comprised a Territorial Headquarters Building (right), a Girl's Dormitory (rear), and a Temple (center).

36. SALVATION ARMY BUILDINGS

B. The interior of the Temple has a ceiling pierced in a willow pattern, through which lights shine.

40. SQUIBB BUILDING
(with Walker & Gillette's FULLER BUILDING [18] behind)

This Fifth Avenue office building of 1929-30 by Ely Jacques Kahn is one of the few buildings he designed that had much of a tower above its setbacks. It is catercornered from Grand Army Plaza and is probably best known to New Yorkers for the F.A.O. Schwartz store on its ground floor.

42. ESSEX HOUSE

Frank Grad's hotel of 1929-30 faces across Central Park South with this composition, which contains a profusion of the volute motif.

43. KENT COLUMBUS CIRCLE GARAGE

Jardine, Hill & Murdock designed some automated parking garages—automatic in the sense that cars were not driven by an attendant after being placed on the buildings' elevators. One was near Grand Central Station. This garage is northwest of Columbus Circle. The shop window is an alteration. The Century Apartments (96) can be seen to the left of the garage.

TELEPHONE BUILDINGS

Throughout the twenties the telephone company was expanding rapidly and put up many new buildings. These three by Voorhees, Gmelin & Walker were all built in 1929-30.

44.
This one, with crystalline forms and zigzags, is on East 13th Street. It is an expansion of an earlier two-story building.

45.

One is on West 17th and 18th Streets west of Seventh Avenue.

46.

A third with faceted forms and willows is on West 50th Street.

48. BEAUX-ARTS APARTMENT HOTEL

These two apartment blocks face each other across 44th Street west of the
UN. They have long been highly regarded by the progressive probably in part
because they were horizontally banded at a time when this was favored by
International Style critics and also presumably because, being on both sides
of the street, they were responsible for a closer-to-total environment than
other, single blocks. They were named after the Beaux-Arts Institute of Design (12) next door. The doormen no longer dress as gendarmes, and the
lobbies have been altered.

49. BARBIZON PLAZA

A and B. This building of 1929-30 by Murgatroyd & Ogden was topped by a glass roof when first built. It still dominates the view north on Sixth Avenue in the Fifties.

50. NATIONAL TITLE GUARANTY COMPANY

Like the Chanin Building (9), this Brooklyn bank building of 1929-30 by Corbett, Harrison & MacMurray has buttresses above its lowest floors. Lamps which were originally in front of the building are no longer there, and the bank interior has been completely altered.

51. NEW SCHOOL FOR SOCIAL RESEARCH

A. Joseph Urban designed this building, the horizontally striped façade of which slopes back to overcome the optical illusion which would make its top appear broader than its bottom. It was built in 1929-30. B and C. Inside, the ceiling of the auditorium, though without stalactites, suggests its parentage in the Berlin Grosses Schauspielhaus of Hans Poelzig. It was described as being formed of perforated plaster.

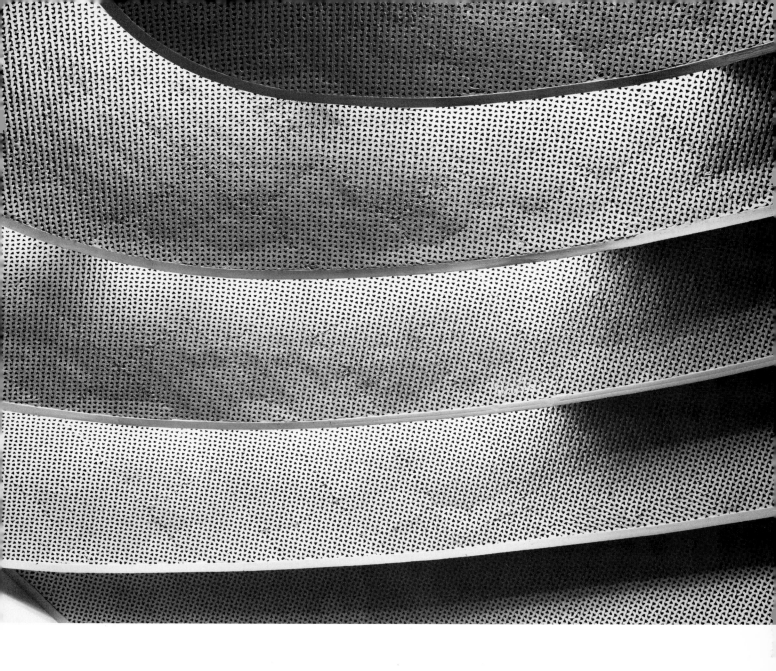

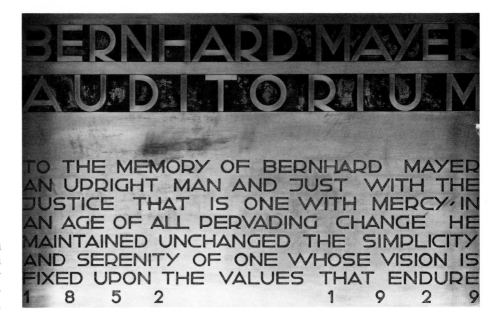

TO THE MEMORY OF BERNHARD MAYER
AN UPRIGHT MAN AND JUST WITH THE
JUSTICE THAT IS ONE WITH MERCY·IN
AN AGE OF ALL PERVADING CHANGE HE
MAINTAINED UNCHANGED THE SIMPLICITY
AND SERENITY OF ONE WHOSE VISION IS
FIXED UPON THE VALUES THAT ENDURE
1 8 5 2   1 9 2 9

D and E. In the auditorium lobby the building's German origins are also suggested by the lettering of the commemorative plaque.

53. SOUTHGATE APARTMENTS

A and B. Two of a variety of entrances to this apartment complex on East 52nd Street next to the river are shown. The buildings were designed by Emery Roth and built in stages from 1929 to 1931.

54. IRVING TRUST BUILDING

A. This bank headquarters building of 1929-32 by Voorhees, Gmelin &
Walker is at the head of Wall Street opposite Trinity Graveyard.

B and C. Its curtain wall is in fabric folds and incised with a fabric pattern.

D. The main banking room has walls and ceilings sheathed in red and gold mosaics designed by Hildreth Meière. E and F. The vault gates and register grills have a sort of pattern that the writer Claude Bragdon suggested the designer generate from magic squares, moves in chess games, and the like.

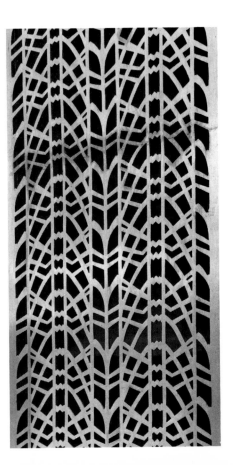

G. At the top of the building's faceted tower appear large windows.

H. The high, faceted-ceilinged lounge within the top of the tower is virtually intact except that the original boldly patterned wall covering has been replaced.

A and B. Sloan & Robertson's brick-sheathed prison in the Village, built in 1929-30, was recently razed.

55. HOUSE OF DETENTION FOR WOMEN

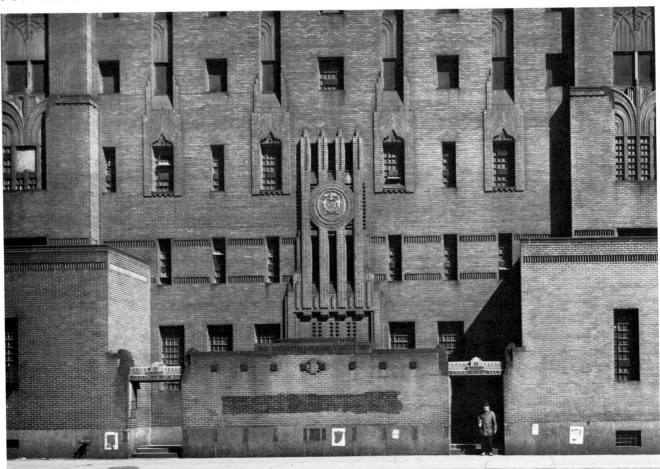

56. BLOOMINGDALE'S

A. In 1930 Bloomingdale's built this extension of their store west to Lexington Avenue. Starrett & Van Vleck were the architects.

B. The first two floors are in black terra-cotta and marble, those above in terra-cotta and brick (now painted). The forms of the terra-cotta may have been inspired by Precolumbian design.

59. CURB EXCHANGE FACADE

This façade was added in 1930 by Starrett & Van Vleck to a pre-existing exchange building just west of Trinity Graveyard. The Curb has since become the American Stock Exchange.

60. TWENTIETH-CENTURY FOX BUILDING

B. Joseph J. Furman was the architect in 1930 of this building on West 56th Street for a Hollywood movie company. Whether or not he was also responsible for the building's interiors is not known. The lobby (see color section) was preserved into the present because for many years its walls were hidden by frames for posters. The movie company has left the building since these pictures were taken.

C. The walls of an upstairs screening room were unfortunately painted over.

61. WEST SIDE ELEVATED HIGHWAY

This roadway, recently much in the news for its present decrepitude, was finished in 1930. John Sloan of Sloan & Robertson had some role in its design. Plaques such as this one were mounted at cross streets to announce the pier beyond and were presumably part of his contribution.

63. 22 EAST 40TH STREET

This office building of 1930 by Kenneth Franzheim was characteristic in that its lower floors, in this case in polished and unpolished black marble, were treated as a sort of stage setting especially related to the street.

APARTMENTS

64.

B and C. A series of apartment houses was built on Central Park West and on the West Side in the years around 1930. This one at 66th Street by Schwartz & Gross had curtain walls of brick which shaded from purple just above the base of the building to yellow at the top (see color section).

65.
A and B. On 86th Street, Margon & Holder also put up a mammoth apartment house at the corner of Amsterdam Avenue, the New Amsterdam.

66.
A and B. A second Schwartz & Gross apartment house at 84th Street and
Central Park West had large sprout-like forms at its base and at its top.

67.
On 86th Street between Central Park West and Columbus Avenue J. M. Felson erected a smaller apartment house with a brick curtain wall and a set of terra-cotta spandrels.

39A and 68A.

On two adjacent blocks farther north, at Central Park West and between 90th and 92nd Streets, Margon & Holder and Emery Roth put up two apartment buildings. One had pointed, fountain-like finials and bronze at its base (39B).

39B.

68 B.
The other had a simpler tower and bands of decorative sandstone and colored concrete skirting its base.

96, 87A and B.

Two Central Park West buildings by the Office of Irwin Chanin, each a block wide, had twin towers and the sort of interlocking fins at their crowns and curved forms behind which would in the thirties be a familiar feature of the design of such products as radios. These were the Century, a few blocks north of Columbus Circle, and the Majestic, across 72nd Street from the Dakota.

87A.

87B.

69. HORN & HARDART

This building for the chain of automated restaurants was built in 1930-31 to designs of Louis Allen Abramson. Standing on 33rd Street near what was Penn Station, it suggests that by this date there was feedback to New York from elsewhere in America. The details here, especially the figures knocking heads on either side of the building, come from the Richfield Building in Los Angeles, whose architects, Morgan, Walls & Clements, apparently got them in turn from Josef Hoffmann's Palais Stoclet in Brussels.

71. RCA VICTOR BUILDING

A. Cross & Cross designed this office tower—now the GE Building—in materials similar in color to those of Saint Bartholmew's Church, which it adjoins. The building to the left is Schultze & Weaver's Waldorf-Astoria (74).

B and C. Above the windows and doors at street level appear zigzag forms presumably representing the vibrating Victrola needles of the RCA Victor Company. The light illuminating the clock and supported by two scrawny arms is, like the GE clock face, a replacement but an Art Deco one.

71C.

Art Deco was the house style of this company, which thereby helped disseminate it throughout the country. This particular building, just south of the General Post Office, was designed by Frank S. Parker and built in 1930-31.

72. SEARS ROEBUCK BUILDING

73. AMERICAN SAVINGS BANK

Irons & Mellor put up this small bank building on 42nd Street between Sixth Avenue and Times Square in 1930-31. It has since ceased to be a bank.

75 and 76. 500 FIFTH AVENUE and
EMPIRE STATE BUILDING

Shreve, Lamb & Harmon were putting up their tower at 500 Fifth Avenue just north of the Public Library in the same years (1930-31) in which their Empire State Building was being erected.

A and B. The Empire State Building passed beyond the early, craft-oriented Art Deco skyscrapers in that many of its forms were made to seem machined and in that its crowning device was functional, if only symbolically so. The building retained the cast metal spandrels of earlier buildings on its exterior.

C. Inside, bridges crossed the lobby. Originally these were not enclosed in glass as they are now, and their ceilings stepped up to a surface from which hung a chandelier.

77. 29 BROADWAY

Sloan & Robertson designed this building for a narrow site towards the very bottom end of Broadway. It was built in 1930-31. A metal screen that hung in the entrance way is no longer in place.

In 1930-31 Ely Jacques Kahn put up two buildings on one block just south of Times Square. One is L-shaped in plan; the other sits within the angle of the L. The first, whose crown appears here at the upper right, faces south.

0 and 81. BRICKEN-CASINO BUILDING and 1400 BROADWAY

The Bricken-Casino building, tucked within the L, asserts itself more stridently with a finned crowning motive and a virtuoso performance in setbacks.

82. McGRAW-HILL BUILDING

C. Below the Mendelsohnian crown, where the lettering has been painted over, columns are sheathed in metal and spandrels are of blue-green terracotta. (See color section.)

B. Raymond Hood's building for the publishing company was built farther west on 42nd Street than other office buildings have been for the reason that zoning would not permit its printing plant closer to the midtown commercial center. Whereas the News Building tower (35) had been designed in the form of a slab perpendicular to the street, the McGraw-Hill has what is virtually a slab parallel to it. The building was built in 1930-31.

83. BROADWAY FASHION BUILDING

This office building with stores on its ground floor is on Broadway just south of 86th Street. It is of the modest sort which characteristically found a place on the Main Streets of most American towns in the thirties, though this one keeps an extra share of elegance by the large amount of glass on its façade in relation to the light framework in which it is set. Sugarman & Berger designed the building, erected in 1930-31.

85. 60 WALL TOWER

A. This office tower of 1930-32 is a block away from its address—it is connected to a Wall Street building by a bridge. Presumably because it became more important in the Depression to rent space than to advertise a company, the building was named after the address rather than the company that built it, Cities Service. Nevertheless, the familiar company logotype is much in evidence. At the entrances there also appears a model of the building. Sculptural models were much used in design in the twenties and thirties; one suspects that both owners and architects hated to do away with them after design was completed, hence such a use as this. The architects here were Holton & George. B. The building is topped with a crystalline lighting fixture.

C. Metal flowers appear above the lobby cigar stand.

D. There are aggressively non-structural corbels at the top of a pilaster in the lobby.

E. The elevator system was innovative in having double-decker cabs, one half of each going to odd floors, the other to even ones, from two lobbies one above the other. The system is common now, but was not profitable in the thirties, and its use was discontinued. Until recently the upper half of some original cabs, such as this one, could be seen.

This building by an architect named Stuckert was built in 1930-32 and represents the Art Deco at its most modest, both in stature and in quality. Originally, rather than holding a Zum Zum's, it housed a Bickford's.

86. LEXINGTON AVENUE AT 45TH STREET

88. EARL CARROLL THEATER

This building, part of honky-tonk west of Rockefeller Center and north of Times Square, was built in 1931 as a theater for demure girlie shows of the day. George Keister was the architect.

89. LONG ISLAND AREA HEADQUARTERS BUILDING

This brick curtain wall with metal window frames set in front of it covers a large telephone company building of 1931 in downtown Brooklyn. Voorhees, Gmelin & Walker designed it. The virtuoso brickwork, as explicitly tapestry-like as any by the firm, also suggests the brickwork of North German Expressionist buildings.

90A. These buildings, all part of the Rockefeller Center complex and built between 1931 and 1935, accounted for most of the construction work undertaken after the Depression had made itself felt. They were designed by several architectural firms working in collaboration and calling themselves the Associated Architects. The setbacks at the sides of the slab of the RCA building are not there in response to the zoning law but to the decreasing number of elevator shafts on the upper floors.

90, 92, 97, 102, 103. RCA BUILDING,
     RADIO CITY MUSIC HALL,
     BRITISH EMPIRE BUILDING,
     MAISON FRANCAISE,
     PALAZZO D'ITALIA,
     INTERNATIONAL BUILDINGS

97A, 102, 103. The row of low blocks on Fifth Avenue (the British, French, Italian, and International buildings) were the Associated Architects' way of relating the Center to the smaller scale of Fifth Avenue. The (former) Time & Life Building (109) is behind them.

90.B. The rear of the Center on Sixth Avenue, where in the thirties there was an elevated railway, shows no such consideration as was shown on Fifth Avenue.

90C. The RCA Building still had the cast metal spandrels of the earlier, craft-oriented Art Deco.

90D, 97B, 90E. Otherwise, the buildings' aesthetic was not a craft one and art was expected to stand on its own. It did not always do so successfully at the Center.

92A and B. The Radio City Music
Hall offered its own complete vision of high life.

92C and D. It also included the
comforts of home.

93. FOURTH CHURCH OF CHRIST SCIENTIST

A and B. Cherry and Matz, specialists in church architecture, did this building in upper Manhattan a few blocks above the George Washington Bridge. It was built in 1931-32 and is at the side of Ft. Washington Park in an area which contains many modest Art Deco apartment houses. The church has recently become a synagogue.

94. METROPOLITAN LIFE, NORTH BUILDING

This large office tower of 1931-32 was, according to early renderings, to have been much higher, a real temple of Babel. It stands between Madison Square and Park Avenue. H. W. Corbett and D. E. Waide were the architects.

95. PROVIDENT LOAN SOCIETY
BRANCH, 72ND STREET

This is one of a great many small loan offices built for this firm. All aim to suggest, by their large-scaled forms, the security of their vaults. Several were done in the Art Deco style by Renwick, Aspinwall & Guard. This one, built in 1932, made way a short while ago for a paint store.

98, 99, 104. CITY OF NEW YORK
SUBSTATIONS

These small buildings are part of the Independent Subway system. Each houses unmanned machinery which converts alternating current into direct current for the subway. The buildings illustrated here were built in 1932 and 1933. The first is near Rockefeller Center, the second in the Village, and the third in Brooklyn.

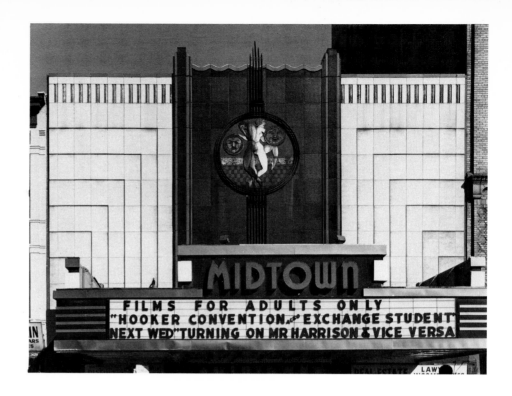

100. MIDTOWN THEATRE

This small movie theater on Broadway above 96th Street was designed by Boak & Paris and built in 1933.

101. FEDERAL OFFICE BUILDING

A. This stone-faced block dating from 1933-35 was designed by Cross & Cross. It stands just north of the new Trade Center buildings and east of the Barclay-Vesey Building (1).

B. At its corners it has an eagle, a flag, and that international nationalist symbol of the time, a fasces.

105. EAST RIVER SAVINGS BANK

This narrow building on Trinity Place just north of the chain of plazas that extends from the Chase Building to the Trade Center was designed by Walker & Gillette and built in 1934-35. The bronze lettering at about eye level on the building has been replaced since this picture was taken by a modish 1970s logotype.

106. KRESS BUILDING

A. This office building and store has a high-ceilinged sales room on its ground floor and several sub-grade floors with a luncheonette and cafeteria. It was designed by Edward Sibbert and built in 1935. B. The decoration on the front is perhaps Mayan in character—each decorative knob depicts a category of merchandise sold in the store.

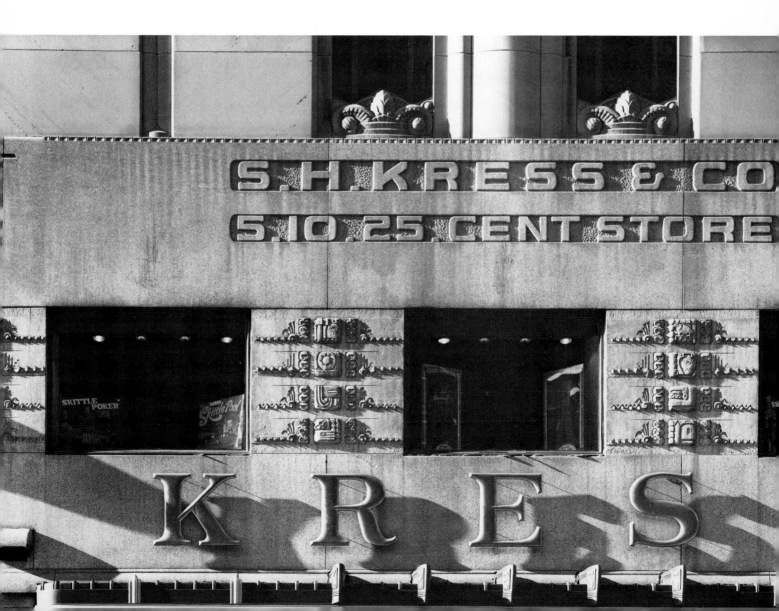

107. PIER BUILDING

This structure, built in 1935, was recently torn down, a casualty of the shift away from ocean liner travel.

108. APARTMENTS, 80TH STREET
AND WEST END

Drape shapes in stainless steel appear at the top of this building of 1935-36
designed by George F. Pelham 2nd.

110. HORN & HARDART, 57TH STREET

This restaurant was designed by Ralph Bencker, a Philadelphia architect who also designed many H & H's in Philadelphia (and the N. W. Ayer Building in that city as well). This New York building, faced in terra-cotta, was built in 1938.

112. CRIMINAL COURTS BUILDING

This structure of 1939 is known as "the Tombs" after its predecessor, a prison in the Egyptian style. It houses both courts and prison and was designed by Harvey Wiley Corbett. It stands just north of Foley Square and backs onto Columbus Park.

113. JOAN OF ARC JUNIOR HIGH SCHOOL

This building in the West Nineties is largely featureless except for this lux-
uriant growth at its entrance. The school was designed by Eric Kebbon and
built in 1939-40.

114. AIRLINES BUILDING

This building, also of 1939-40, only recently ceased to serve its original purpose as an airlines ticket office. It was designed (by John B. Peterkin) to serve a number of other uses as well. It still houses a garage in its basement and was meant to have, as well as restaurants, a theater in space that has long been occupied by a Horn & Hardart.

115. TIFFANY BUILDING

A and B. By the time Cross & Cross designed this building (erected in 1939-40) at the corner of Fifth Avenue and 57th Street, the Art Deco had largely returned to the classical forms it had originated in. The Fuller Building (18) appears to the left of it in A, the Stewart store (25) (now Bonwit Teller) to the right in B.

PHOTO CREDITS

Permission to reprint material from copyright sources among the following is gratefully acknowledged:

Eliel Saarinen, Chicago Tribune Building competition entry, from *The International Competition for a New Administration Building for the Chicago Tribune, MCMXXII* (Chicago: The Tribune Company, 1923), Plate Number 13.

Helmle & Corbett, zoning envelope studies, renderings by Hugh Ferriss, from Harvey Wiley Corbett, "Zoning and the Envelope of the Building," *Pencil Points*, 4 (April 1923), 16.

McKenzie, Voorhees & Gmelin, Barclay-Vesey Building, plan, and Helmle, Corbett & Harrison and Sugarman & Berger, Master Building, plan, from Plate 8, Part II of Volume I, and Plate 4, Part VII of Volume III of *American Architecture of the 20th Century*, Oliver Reagan, ed. (New York: The Architectural Book Publishing Company).

Buchman & Kahn, Insurance Center Building, photograph of model, from *American Architect*, 129 (April 20, 1926), 454.

Joseph Urban, Ziegfeld Theater, photograph by Sigurd Fischer from *Architectural Record*, 61 (May 1927), 388.

William Van Alen, Chrysler Building, plan, from *Architectural Forum*, 53 (October 1930), 412.

Howells & Hood, 3 East 84th Street, rendering by Donald Douglas, *Pencil Points*, 8 (November 1927), 660.

Howells & Hood, News Building, plans, *Architectural Forum*, 53 (November 1930), 542

L. H. Boileau, Bon Marché Pavilion, and J. Hiriard, Tribout & Beau, Pavilion of the Galéries Lafayette from M. Roux-Spitz, *Exposition des Arts Décoratifs Paris 1925* (Paris: Albert Lévy, 1928), plates 52 and 54.

Josef Hoffmann, Palais Stoclet, general exterior and dining room, from Josef Hoffmann, *Wendingen* (Amsterdam: "de Hooge Brug," 1920), pp. 4, 11.

Josef Hoffmann, Palais Stoclet, exterior detail, and Eric Mendelsohn's sketches for industrial buildings, from Sheldon Cheney, *The New World Architecture* (New York, 1930), pp. 182, 96.

Interior of Wiener Werkstätte, by Joseph Urban, New York, from *Architectural Record*, 53 (March 1923), p. 269.

César Klein, Bedroom for Wolfgang Gurlitt, Berlin, from *Junge Kunst*, 5 (1923), n.p.

Walter Gropius, Sommerfeld House, Berlin, stairwell and door, from *Staatliches Bauhaus Weimar 1919-1923* (Weimar and Munich: Bauhausverlag, 1923), ill. 117 and 45.

Scene from *Dr. Mabuse*, from Siegfried Kracauer, *From Caligari to Hitler* (Princeton, N.J.: Princeton University Press, hardback reprint ed., 1966), ill. 6.

Fritz Höger, Chilehaus, Hamburg, general view, from Gustav Adolf Platz, *Die Baukunst der Neuesten Zeit* (Berlin: Propyläen-Verlag, 1930), plate XI.

Fritz Höger, Chilehaus, detail, from *Moderne Bauformen*, 24 (1925), plate 15.

Peter Behrens, I. G. Farben, Höchst, main hall, from Paul Joseph Cremers, *Peter Behrens—Sein Werk von 1909 bis zur Gegenwart* (Essen: G. D. Baedeker Verlag, 1928), plate 7.

Hans Poelzig, Grosses Schauspielhaus, Berlin, foyer, from *Wasmuths Monatshefte für Baukunst* (1920-21), plate 14.

Frank Lloyd Wright, Midway Gardens, Chicago, detail from *Architectural Record*, 62 (Dec. 1927), 454.

Frank Lloyd Wright, A. D. German Warehouse, Richland Center, Wisconsin, and Hollyhock House, Hollywood, from Henry-Russell Hitchcock, *In the Nature of Materials 1887-1941—The Buildings of Frank Lloyd Wright* (New York: Duell, Sloan, and Pearce, 1942), ill. 204, 235. Better illustrations of the Wright buildings would have been used if difficulties raised by the Taliesin Foundation, which retains copyright on much Wright material, had not prevented it.

Scenes from Robert Wiene's *The Cabinet of Dr. Caligari* and scenes from Fritz Lang's *Metropolis*, courtesy of The Museum of Modern Art, New York, Film Stills Archive).

The color photographs of the Chrysler Building were first published in *Architecture PLUS* (May-June 1974).